The more I st[udy]
more I stand amazed at the
work of the Creator — Louis Pasteur

May all your days be filled with
sunshine and all your wishes come true.
With friendship,
Gloria Smith

Bloom Where You
Are Appointed

Bloom Where You Are Appointed

GLORIA SMITH

Library of Congress Control Number:		2009908065
ISBN:	Hardcover	978-1-4415-6276-0
	Softcover	978-1-4415-6275-3

Note: Scripture quotations are the author's paraphrase based on the King James version of the Bible.

This book was printed in the United States of America.

To order additional copies of this book, contact:
Xlibris Corporation
1-888-795-4274
www.Xlibris.com
Orders@Xlibris.com
65998

Contents

For Joe

whose deep and abiding love has always been
the wind beneath my wings.

ACKNOWLEDGMENTS

JUST AS NO man is an island, no woman is an island either. I owe a debt to many people. After meeting thousands of people in my journey, I had the opportunity to share many people's life experiences. Many of the people in my stories are deceased, and some of the people's names have been changed to protect their privacy. Still, they impressed me in some way, and they added depth to my life, along with friendship and love.

I owe a special debt to my husband, Joe, who preached stimulating sermons that were uplifting to me as well as to other people. He stood by me in sickness and in health. His daily sense of humor helped me not dwell on the cloudy moments in life.

I owe a debt to all my family who give me their support and unconditional love.

I owe a debt to my writing coach, book author and college instructor, David Biscoff, who has encouraged me to continue writing.

I owe a debt of appreciation to David Craft who gave me his release of copyright on our family pictures.

I owe a special thanks to Dyess-Tidwell studio for their permission to print copies of a couple of professional pictures in this book.

I owe a debt to all the people who said, "Gloria, you should write a book." Thank you, dear friends, for the encouragement. I did it!

I Believe

I believe in the brook as it wanders
From hillside into glade;
I believe in the breeze as it whispers
When evening's shadows fade.
I believe in the cry of the tempest'
Mid the thunder's cannonade.

I believe in the light of shining stars,
I believe in the sun and the moon;
I believe in the flash of lightning,
I believe in the night – bird's croon.
I believe in the faith of the flowers,
I believe in the rock and sod,
For in all of these appeareth
Clear handiwork of God.

– Author unknown

PREFACE

Joe was called to the ministry by a nightmare.

Early one morning at the beginning of his senior year in high school, he woke up sweating. He had dreamed that he was trying to make a sermon and was doing a terrible job of it. This was odd because Joe had already decided to become a contractor and build houses. He couldn't understand why he'd have such a dream.

Weeks went by, and Joe couldn't get the nightmare out of his mind. It became a kind of secret obsession. Over and over, it rolled through his thoughts. He kept asking himself, "Do I want to be a minister? Is that why I had this nightmare?" He considered telling his parents about the dream but was afraid his dad would laugh.

He decided to talk with his own pastor, Reverend Adams, who encouraged him to answer the call. "The ministry needs young men like you," the older man told him.

When Joe finally spoke to his parents about the dream and how he was thinking of becoming a minister, his dad didn't laugh as he had expected. In fact, his parents pledged their support.

Joe received a license to preach in 1955 while he was still a senior in high school. He would need four years of college and three years of seminary to become an ordained Methodist minister.

After a year at Young Harris College in the north Georgia mountains, Joe transferred to Florida Southern College in Lakeland, Florida. While there, he accepted a student appointment at the Eaton Park Methodist Church. With good instructors in the college religion department and the experience of serving a small church, Joe felt that he would be ready for seminary.

Joe graduated from college in June 1959 and went back to work in his hometown. The First United Methodist Church of Moultrie, Georgia, needed him for the summer as an assistant pastor and youth minister.

On Joe's second Sunday back in his home church, a young lady walked in. Gloria Manning had recently moved to Moultrie from Thomasville, Georgia, where she had attended a private Methodist girls school. She was now enrolled in a local nursing school connected with Norman College. Joe wasted no time in asking this new girl in town for a date. He told his parents, "She is the most beautiful girl that I have ever met, and just her smile will light up anyone's life!" They agreed.

Joe soon left for seminary at Emory University in Atlanta, but he kept in touch with the girl he planned to marry. By December 20, 1959, Joe had convinced the young lady to be his bride. Joe and Gloria had a lovely wedding at the church where they first met.

While in seminary, Joe was given a student appointment, the Kite charge. The charge had four churches, three in the country and one in the small town of Kite, Georgia.

If seminary was a piece of cake, then this student appointment was the icing on the cake. It would prepare Joe and Gloria for ministry and parsonage living.

This book is about a couple's forty-year journey through ministry. They encounter challenges in their personal lives as they move from one place to another. Their main goal is to *bloom where they are appointed!* They do this by helping other people face the challenges and setbacks in life as well as rejoicing with them over the victories in life. Life never stays the same, and it requires knowing how to move on after suffering a setback or winning a victory.

This, then, is their story.

EMORY UNIVERSITY AND THE KITE CHARGE: 1960-1962

W<small>E SAT FOR</small> a while and looked at the rusty tin roof, peeling white paint, rickety wooden steps, and the porch where spiderwebs covered the rocking chairs. In the yard were moss-covered oaks and naked pecan trees.

We had just driven up to our first home together, and I said to my new husband, "Joe, this house can't be the parsonage!"

So began my life with a young Methodist minister.

I had been Gloria Manning.

Now I was Mrs. Joe Smith.

Who was I then?

Growing up, I heard people say I was beautiful so much that I sometimes believed them. Of course, it pleases any girl to be admired, so I smiled a lot in spite of my unhappy childhood. I had dark brown hair, big brown eyes, and smooth, suntanned skin. Looking back, I think of the song in *The Sound of Music* that says, "Somewhere in my youth or childhood, I must have done something good."

While in high school, I knew I could not always get by with just my looks, so I became an honor student. I decided I wanted to go to college after high school.

With my bright smile and my love for people, I appeared very confident and acted older than my age. Underneath the smile was an insecure young woman. In spite of my insecurities, I wanted to reach for the stars and prove myself to the world. I was definitely very ambitious. I was very active in high school playing softball and volleyball. But my main interests were music (singing) and drama (stage plays). After getting the starring role in the senior play, I definitely was starstruck!

While at the private girls' school, I became a soft spoken, ladylike young woman; and no one could have guessed that I had ever been a tomboy. I had enjoyed hunting, fishing, and playing softball with my brothers and their friends before going to the girls' school. I was in the tenth grade when I entered the boarding school.

At the boarding school, I was a leader in many campus activities including the religious activities. I was also a leader in the youth activities at the Methodist Church where I had joined shortly after arriving at the boarding school.

"Two roads diverged in a wood and I took the one less traveled by and that has made all the difference." I remember those lines from the poem "The Road Not Taken" by Robert Frost. My belief in a personal god was my strength and my guidance. I silently prayed often for guidance, and I know that must have made a big difference in my life. With my actions, I let other people know that I was a Christian girl, and I didn't intend to stumble down any wrong paths. I look back and thank that young girl for the paths not taken. My actions got me lots of encouragement from some of my teachers and ministers and respect from my peers.

Now though, beside those pecan trees, looking at where I was supposed to live, I wasn't so sure about things.

My husband, Joe Smith, laughed. "Spooky, isn't it? Pecan trees always look dead in the winter. Things will look better in spring when the pecan trees get new leaves and we give the house a new coat of paint during spring break."

Being a new bride of just a few weeks, I said, "Well, what are we sitting here for? Aren't you going to carry me over the threshold? It's time to see the inside of our house. Maybe we'll be surprised by some inside beauty."

With a cheerful smile, Joe opened the car door. "No one can say I'm not a Southern gentleman."

Joe was a nice-looking young man with black hair, hazel eyes, and olive skin. He seemed confident about himself except he wished he could have been taller. His short-guy appearance didn't seem to hinder his popularity with the young women who knew him. He had a very outgoing personality and with a good sense of humor. Joe was the type of fellow liked by everyone, his peers as well as his elders. As a teenager, Joe was more athletic than studious. He played football and baseball, and he liked to swim and water ski. Also, he enjoyed biking and hiking.

He went to church with his family, and they were Baptist until they all left the Baptist Church and joined the Methodist Church while Joe was still a teenager. Joe was very impressed with his Methodist minister and that impression helped him decide to become a minister. Joe became dedicated and loyal to the Methodist Church.

Joe went away to college with high ambitions. He became a more serious student while in college and just occasionally went skiing and swimming. With studies and work, he didn't have time for sports.

Joe was a faithful and dedicated Christian and a loyal Methodist without acting pious about his faith.

Now, as Joe, my new husband, tried to carry me across the threshold of our new parsonage, events illustrated that as wonderful as he was, he was all too human.

We made it halfway up the rotten front steps when – CRASH! – down to the ground we fell! Joe had dropped his bride! Thank goodness there were no broken bones. We laughed until we cried.

The next day, the news got around town. Across the street from the Methodist parsonage, the Baptist neighbor had watched the whole scene from her kitchen window. For years, the neighbor had watched the bachelor ministerial students come and go. But now they had a couple, and the parsonage steps were inadequate!

The talk among the Baptists was "Shame on the Methodist! The new pastor and his bride didn't make it safely up the rotten parsonage steps!"

But the Baptists didn't shame the Methodists for long.

First, the Methodist bricklayer came to the parsonage.

"Preacher," he said, "they tell me you need some new front steps." By the end of the day, he had built some beautiful brick steps.

After seeing me unpacking our wedding china, the churchwomen bought a new china cabinet. In her sweet Southern accent, Mrs. Powell said, "Oh, honey, your bridal china is too nice for this old antique pie safe. We'll store it in the garage."

"I don't mind the old safe, but the new china cabinet is really lovely! Thank you so much."

I was expressing sincere appreciation.

When spring arrived, the yard did look much better with green grass and new leaves on the nice, shady pecan trees.

By the end of summer, we had painted the whole seven-room house inside and out, even the tin roof! I was sure Joe was going to slide down the steep tin roof, and that would be the end of my future babies. Standing under the old oak tree, I kept yelling, "Joe, please hold on. Be careful!"

Joe kept painting and singing "If I Were a Rich Man," similar to a song from the musical *Fiddler on the Roof,* as I tensely watched and wished we were just rich enough to hire a painter.

Later inside the house, I was painting the trim when I noticed that Joe had finished the walls of an entire room while I still had miles to go before the trim was done. "I think I've got the hardest part of painting a room," I complained.

Joe smiled. "I knew you'd picked the most tedious part of a painting job, but you're good at it. I'm not."

"So I'm good at it, you say. Flattery will get you a million brownie points, right?" I was teasing him.

My twelve-year-old sister, Lois, had summer vacation from boarding school, and she helped with the parsonage projects too. Besides painting, we cleaned the house and yard, and we put vegetables in the freezer. When Joe visited farmers, they were always generous, sharing vegetables with their pastor. They had wonderful corn, peas, beans, and some of the best watermelons in the country.

Before that summer was over, I received an important letter from the Glenn County Juvenile Court judge asking me, "Would you like to accept the custody of your sister, Lois?" I was only twenty years old, but I accepted the custody of my sister. With Lois, Joe and I were now a family of three.

That fall, we took Lois back to boarding school in Thomasville, and we returned to Emory University in Atlanta. During the week, we lived on campus in one of the married dorms, and on weekends, we drove over a hundred miles back to the Kite parsonage. Thank God for youth and lots of energy!

While Joe was busy with seminary classes, I worked at the seminary and took noncredit night courses. These were offered to adults in the community who wanted to take some religion courses taught by the seminary professors. So this gave me the opportunity to experience some of the same professors that Joe had in his day classes.

Joe and I had lots of discussions about religions of mankind, a course about different religions.

It was a wonderful way to keep us close.

But it also kept my mind sharp for other things.

"The professors are nice to work for, but I'm glad that I'm not planning to be a secretary all my life," I told Joe.

Joe said, "After I finish seminary, then you'll have time to go back and finish your degree."

I had planned to finish my degree before marriage, but life with Joe seemed more exciting, living in the big city of Atlanta at Emory University, instead of the small private college where I was spending the last year of my teens.

During a meeting with the other young wives at the seminary, one remarked, "This is the way we earn our PHT [put hubby through] degree, by working while our husbands are in school."

On Sundays, I noticed Joe saying "watn't" and "dodn't" in his sermons. Never on a Sunday, but on Monday I said, "Please, Joe, say 'does not' or 'was not' or at least 'doesn't' or 'wasn't' in your sermons. You made an A in English grammar, so you know better than 'dodn't' and 'watn't'!"

Joe had grown up in South Georgia hearing words spoken that way, and he wasn't about to give them up for any proper professor or even his wife. Those two words and a Southern accent were a part of him, and he kept them for the rest of his ministry, along with some brilliantly prepared sermons. With his natural sense of humor, Joe always kept his congregations entertained.

Joe didn't want to impress people with sesquipedalian terms, so he didn't use words that are a foot and a half long. He would rather impress people with a sermon on the historical view of the Bible.

"I just want people to understand my sermons and go home with something that will help improve their understanding of God and Christian living," he told me.

Weekends, we were on the road again. There were sermons to preach and board meetings, funeral services, and weddings to attend. Sometimes in the middle of the week, Joe had to leave seminary classes and go back to Kite for a funeral. The seminary professors were always understanding about giving a missed-class test at a later date.

With this four-circuit charge, there was lots of work: sick members to visit, programs to plan, needy children to help, and church family dinner dates to remember. Also, at the parsonage, there was grass to mow and a dusty house to clean!

Often, Joe begged me to leave my housework and go visiting with him. "The people love you so much, and they seem so disappointed when I call on them without you," he said.

He finally convinced me to go with him when he said, "A hundred years from now, it will not matter if the house is dusty." After all, we were now a team together in ministry.

There were families and friends to entertain. The revival ministers came in the summer. Every year, each church planned a week-long revival. After going to those four revivals and eating big country dinners with members each night for a month, Joe and I didn't feel revived. We were exhausted!

One Saturday night, a middle-aged man and woman came to the parsonage door, asking for a quick wedding. First, Joe talked with them, and then he agreed to marry them. Before the vows could be completed, the groom passed out on the living room floor. After I helped the bride revive her groom, and he was standing again, Joe went on with the wedding vows.

Would life always be this busy? we wondered. School and work were preparing us for congregations in the future. It would get busier. Also, we learned that some people are not easily pleased. Impossible expectations have to be ignored. Let God deal with them, and life goes on. Maybe that's why some people make the statement, "I wouldn't want to trade places with a minister and his wife. There are too many people to please."

One fall, the Kite Elementary School had their usual Halloween fair; and the town palm reader, who also attended our church, was asked to tell fortunes as one of the amusement activities. The people called her the real fortune-teller. I was curious, and just for fun, I had her read my hand.

The fortune-teller looked at my hand. "You will have two children, a boy and a girl. You will always be a faithful friend, especially to your family, and you will be the woman behind a very successful man. Together, you will go a long way in life. There will be high steeple churches in your future. And there will always be lots of friends and people in your life."

"That sounds good to me." I smiled as I thanked the fortune-teller. Later, Joe laughed and said, "I thought she was supposed to tell you that you would write best-selling novels, and we would someday be rich!"

"I'll leave the writing to you. It's your job to write good sermons. If I've got to listen to the same preacher the rest of my life, he better be good!"

He laughed.

Back at the seminary, I noticed a friendly black man who often walked down the hall, shaking hands with students changing classes. One day he stopped to speak to me at my desk. He shook my hand and said, "If your husband is going to be a minister, he'll always need the support of his wife. May God bless you and your husband."

I was impressed, yet puzzled. After all, it was the early sixties, and the seminary students and professors were all white.

"Joe, there's a black man who walks up and down the hall, shaking hands as the students change classes? He's friendly and confident, and he's always well dressed in a suit. Who is he?"

"Oh, that's one of Atlanta's black ministers," Joe said. "I guess he's recruiting friends for his cause. His name is Martin Luther King, Jr."

Life went on as usual at the seminary, with few seeming to realize they were being challenged by a man with a cause that would change American society.

Someday, children would read about him in their history books.

One weekend, back at the Kite charge, we learned how a minister can get caught up in a feud between brothers.

One of the churches put a list every month on the bulletin board with the date and name of the family inviting the minister and his wife for Sunday dinner. This was a longtime social custom in this community. For the host family, it was an event! Sometimes, the hostess skipped church, finishing the meal after she had spent days baking pies and cakes. This was before Crock-Pots and microwave ovens.

Before church started that Sunday morning, Joe looked on the bulletin board to find out who was having us for dinner. The Turner family was listed for that Sunday. Well, there were two Turner families in the church. Which one? Joe would find out by asking them later.

After church, as Joe was shaking hands at the door, Charles Turner said, "Come on over to the house. My wife is expecting you all for dinner."

A few seconds later, Ben Turner walked by and said, "Come on up to the house, my wife is expecting y'all for dinner."

Joe explained that his brother had already given an invitation to his house. Maybe Gloria and I can eat with you and your wife next Sunday."

Now, these were *feuding* brothers. They attended the same church but hadn't spoken in years. They had not peacefully settled the family farm after their parents died. Ben Turner said, "Preacher, I can't excuse you from dinner because my wife is home expecting you."

My glance at Joe, with raised eyebrows, asked, *How do you settle this one, my love?*

Without missing a beat, Joe said, "Okay, Mr. Ben, tell your wife we'll be there shortly."

Joe walked over to the other brother. "Mr. Charles, please explain to your wife that Gloria and I will be a little late for dinner. I have pressing church business to take care of first."

The agreeable brother smiled. "Sure, she'll understand."

After eating with the Ben Turners, we politely excused ourselves to go over to the other brother's house for another dinner. That Sunday, Joe ate two full dinners, but I took very small helpings.

When we got home, Joe took some Alka Seltzer tablets. This was a Sunday dinner to remember. We talked about the experience until it got funny, and we had a good, long laugh over our two meals. But isn't it sad that brothers break their relationship over a family farm, a little earthly dirt?

Later, I took a literature course and made an A writing up the "Brother's Feud" story. Even bad experiences are good for something! Thanks to the Turner brothers, I had a story to tell.

Of course, the church is not exempt from imperfect people. Ministers hear the remark, "I don't go to church because the church is filled with hypocrites!"

But there are imperfect people outside of the church as well.

Thank goodness most church members are good, respectable people.

On a cold winter night in February, Joe and I had just arrived at the Kite parsonage from Atlanta when the phone rang.

It was Mr. Wheeler!

"You young folks must be tired and hungry," said Mr. Wheeler. "Come on out to the farm. I have oyster stew on the stove. It's not much, but it'll warm y'all up."

"Sure, Mr. Wheeler. We'll be there as soon as we unload the car."

It was like going home to Granddaddy's farm. Mr. Wheeler was a widower, and his children were grown with homes of their own. But Mr. Wheeler still kept an orderly and welcoming home.

When Joe and I arrived, we were seated in the kitchen to chat with Mr. Wheeler as he stirred a delicious smelling stew. The wood floors had been scrubbed. The long kitchen table with homemade benches had once served a large family. Now, it was set with soup bowls and a huge bowl of saltine crackers.

The coffee pot was perking on the wood stove, which gave the kitchen a warm, cozy smell. This tired young couple was grateful for the warm, homey atmosphere with good food and some special conversation. Mr. Wheeler said, "Joe, can you bless this meal for us?"

I wasn't sure if it was the white hair and the sparkle in his gray eyes or just the way he expressed himself that made Mr. Wheeler seem like an old, respected philosopher. He spoke wisely about how he had lived and raised his family. The successful careers of his children proved that he had been a good father because Mr. Wheeler's sons didn't grow up to be cowboys.

"I always encouraged my children to appreciate learning, and I encouraged them to seek a good education. John is a lawyer in Atlanta." He proudly named each child and told of their careers in teaching, business, and social work.

"They all did fine, and I'm proud of them. When my wife's sister died, we took in her three children and raised them too. And we never thought of it as a burden, only glad that we were blessed with enough strength to do it. We took them to church and Sunday school. They were good children."

He continued telling his life's story. "The thirty-acre farm and my school bus driving job was enough for us to get by. Every summer, we took the children on a special trip. One summer, we took them to Washington DC to see the White House and the Capitol building."

This man had lost his wife but not his faith. He knew how to make the best of life under some difficult circumstances. If you had the choice to sit down with a professor or Mr. Wheeler, you might learn as much or more from Mr. Wheeler than from some professors. Mr. Wheeler's life showed you that there really is light at the end of a dark tunnel.

After the supper with Mr. Wheeler, Joe teased me. "There's one thing that fools Mr. Wheeler. He thinks his minister's wife walks on angel's dust."

"He's the grandfather I always wanted. You're lucky to have known your grandfathers. One of mine was dead before I was born, and the other one died when I was too young to remember him."

Joe and I appreciated Mr. Wheeler and would always remember his hospitality and love.

On February 20, 1962, Joe and I watched John Glenn orbit the earth. We watched this event on television at the Emory University married dorm.

It was a historical moment!

The United States was working hard to be the leader of the world's adventures in space. We were in a rush to get ahead of the Soviet Union. John Glenn made the orbit just ten days after Soviet cosmonaut Yuri Gagarin became the first man in space, making one trip around the globe. Now, John Glenn had made three orbits around the earth. Joe and I were very interested in mankind's adventures exploring the heavens.

#

Ms. Judy was the teacher for the Kite church adult Sunday school class. She was a retired elementary school teacher, and one could tell that she missed her position, especially the opportunity for disciplining other people. Some teachers extend the habit of critiquing and disciplining children to other adults. She showed her bossy personality big-time when she became upset, not only with the younger members of her Sunday school class, but also with the minister and his wife. She was not happy that they planned a picnic and swim party on a Sunday afternoon. She told her class that parading around in bathing suits and partying on Sunday afternoon was downright sinful.

It seemed her idea of a perfect Sunday afternoon was staying home to read the Bible and just visiting with family and neighbors. No picnics, no movies, no parties.

Boring!

Of course, the minister and his church group had their swim party without Ms. Judy or her permission.

Not only did Ms. Judy teach Sunday school, but she also played the piano for the church service. And she played the hymns with a fast honky-tonk touch. It was bearable, like getting used to bugs on a picnic.

Classical church music was not her choice of music.

Anyway, her old-fashioned conservatism was a thorn in the flesh for a young minister. He just kept his personal opinions to himself and gave her the senior respect she deserved. Dealing with her type was a learning experience. But a young minister could look forward to more sophisticated leadership in future churches, he hoped.

It seems like difficult people are always around, whether in business, politics, or the church. Some are a lot worse than a Ms. Judy. Without disagreeable people, we would have a peaceful world.

After Joe had preached at three churches and I had listened to the same sermon three times, a television show was a well-earned chance to relax. Each Sunday night, we watched a favorite show – *Bonanza*!

Monday mornings were the time to pack and make the trip back to Atlanta. The seminary did not have classes on Mondays because so many of the students had weekend church jobs. Classes began again on Tuesdays. I went back to work on Tuesdays too.

A young girl from a poor family in the Kite church was going away to a city to work and find a better life for herself. She was excited as she told me about her ambitions of becoming a singer and looking for a nightclub singing job while she made her way working as a waitress. She was still a teenager and had just finished high school. I warned her that life may not always be easy for a young girl alone in a big city. I shared with her a little poem that I hoped would help her make some right choices along the way.

MYSELF
by Edgar Albert Guest

I have to live with myself, and so,
I want to be fit for myself to know;
I want to be able as days go by
Always to look myself straight in the eye;
I don't want to stand with the setting sun
And hate myself for the things I've done.

I don't want to keep on a closet shelf
A lot of secrets about myself,
And fool myself as I come and go
Into thinking that nobody else will know
The kind of person I really am;
I don't want to dress myself up in shame.

I never can hide myself from me,
I see what others may never see,
I know what others may never know,
I never can fool myself – and so,
Whatever happens, I want to be,
Self-respecting and conscience free.

One week, we were called back to Kite by a family fighting to save their only son. They had four older daughters, and Billy was born last. His parents and older sisters were so proud of him. They had spoiled him with so much attention and love. In his family's eyes, Billy was the perfect young son and brother. But now, at fourteen years old, he was in the hospital with bacterial meningitis. The family wanted their minister to visit him in the hospital and say a prayer by his bedside.

I sat in the hallway at the hospital as I watched Joe robe himself in a hospital gown and mask before going into the highly infectious room. It was sad that such a young boy was so seriously ill, and I felt the pain of the parents and older sisters. But I also felt the fear of my husband being exposed to such a dreaded illness.

The next day, the young man died. His funeral was so sad. At the graveside, one sister cried so hard she fainted, and another young teenage sister had to be pulled away from her brother's coffin. She screamed as uncles pulled her back to a waiting car. Of course, the parents were heartbroken, and other family members were trying to comfort them as well. It was the saddest and most emotional funeral that I had ever experienced in my young life. Joe and I followed the family home afterward and did the best we could to comfort all of them.

A few days later, I went to the doctor for a checkup and found out I was pregnant. Again, I worried about Joe going into the contagious hospital room. Now I had my unborn baby to protect from such dreadful illnesses as meningitis. I had heard people talking and saying how easily bacterial meningitis could spread to other family members and to anyone who came in contact with an ill person. I was so relieved when no one else came down with that dreaded illness.

Mark was born four months before Joe finished seminary. No baby could have been more welcomed to the world! The Kite charge showered him with 343 visits, many gifts, and love. You would have thought he was the most famous and the most beautiful baby in the world! He had a head full of black hair like his dad and dark eyes like his mother. He was kissed and held so much that I was afraid he would catch pneumonia.

Joe finished seminary, and it was time to move on. Other pastures were calling a young pastor and his family to Homestead, Florida. Even though we were excited about moving and looked forward to the possibilities ahead, Joe and I felt sad that we were leaving the dear people on the Kite charge.

The people waved goodbye, and many of the women and children cried as their beloved minister and his family drove away from the Kite parsonage. We had shared three years of our lives with the Kite people, and the people had loved us. That love was mutual. Joe and I had given ourselves to the people, but it seemed as if we had received twice as much as we had given. Could we really love another group of people the way we had grown to love these dear people? Time would tell.

HOMESTEAD, FLORIDA: 1962-1965

AFTER PASSING THE Florida line, I remembered a childhood game that my grade school classmates and I had played. It was a little guessing game about futures: where would we live, how many children would we have, and what career would we choose. I always wrote down Florida as the place I wanted to live. Now I felt like my childhood dream was coming true!

Joe was pleased that I would like Florida. "After attending Florida Southern College in Lakeland, I always knew I wanted to return to Florida," he said.

We stopped at a park by the side of the road in Leesburg, Florida, to enjoy the delicious picnic that Joe's mother had packed for us. We had stopped for an overnight visit with Joe's parents before leaving Georgia. They had stood waving goodbye in the driveway with sad faces, as if we were taking their grandbaby to another country.

In the picnic basket were fried chicken, homemade biscuits, pimento cheese sandwiches, sweet ice tea, pound cake, and baby food for Mark.

That was the day I envisioned the Cracker Barrel Restaurant chain.

"Joe, wouldn't a restaurant that serves this kind of food along the highway be a hit with travelers?"

"Keep dreaming! Remember, I'm just a preacher man. If we had a restaurant, you would be the upfront hostess, and I would be the one back in the kitchen, cooking fish and washing dishes."

"Oh, yeah, and I'm just the girl next door who gave up the good life to be a preacher's wife. And my drama teacher wanted me to go to drama school in New York. Just think, by now my name might be up in lights. And I gave it all up for you and baby Mark." I was lovingly looking down at my beautiful sleeping baby as I teased my husband. Then I added, "I wouldn't trade my nomadic life as a preacher's wife and a mother for all the lights in New York.'

Joe turned serious as he said, "I don't expect you to be a preacher's wife. I just need you to be *my* wife."

At that moment, I came to terms with knowing that I could never be the typical minister's wife. I didn't have the image. I didn't even play the piano. I would just have to be myself, the girl next door who loved stylish clothes and practical things. But I would always be reaching for some impossible dreams, making some of them possible. I wanted to continue my education and earn my college degree.

Back in the car, we continued the drive down the winding roads to South Florida. We must have been a sight to behold in our little black Volkswagen, pulling a little trailer with our few earthly belongings. We were on our way to pastures unknown.

The Smith family arrived! We saw the beautiful royal palms that lined the main street of Homestead. Where's the church? It was just a few miles out of town, in the Redlands! The Redlands farming area had miles and miles of tomato fields, beans, and strawberry fields. In those fields, strawberries grew bigger than thumb tomatoes! The papaya and mango trees sure looked different from Georgia peach trees, and the fruits tasted strange to us. We were used to the taste of watermelons and peaches.

We found the parsonage in town.

It was a modern little three-bedroom house with sheer white curtains that blew from the open windows like billowing white clouds on a spring day. It was January, but there were no signs of winter with the warm breezes and sunshine. The clean, furnished house seemed to welcome a tired family.

We soon learned there was so much humidity that it meant taking several baths a day until we adjusted to the change in climate. Along with the humidity, there were mosquitoes as big as cow flies! Joe sprayed himself with insect repellant before knocking on the doors of his new church members. The pests flew out of the hedges by the dozens.

It was a beautiful, strange land indeed. On the phone, Joe told his parents, "It really looks like the world might be flat after all. There isn't one hill in sight, but we can easily ride our bikes all over town on Sunday afternoons."

Sure, later the hurricanes would come. But right now, life was new and sometimes lonely without old friends and family, yet it was tinged with new excitement.

Moves would always include some moments of loneliness as old friends and familiar surroundings were left behind, and we concentrated on the task of cultivating new friends and adjusting to new faces and places.

Joe said, "Just think. We have warm sunshine in Homestead while our friends and relatives in Georgia are still having cold weather."

The members at the Redland church were mostly farmers and military families. A few had businesses in town. They welcomed us with an old-fashioned pounding party. They came with pounds of everything, including a delicious homemade pound cake.

A farmer teased, "We thought you might miss your Georgia grits." A cute petite couple with New Jersey accents brought a pound of butter. All of the gifts were pounds of basic items that a young family could use.

Joe and I expressed our appreciation. Later, I looked over the loaded dining room table and wondered, "Where will I store all these pounds of food in my small kitchen with no pantry?" At least the old Georgia parsonage had plenty of storage room. I was homesick. I missed Georgia and the people I had grown to love.

Joe had made a great first impression though. He loved his new congregation, and they thought he was sent from heaven

The first Sunday at the Redland church, Joe introduced me and baby Mark to the congregation. After the introduction, he added, "Well, we are adjusting quite nicely to beautiful Homestead, only Gloria is having a hard time finding her peach nut snuff."

Of course, the congregation loved that bit of humor even if it was at the expense of their proper-looking young minister's wife.

Now this is the rest of the snuff story. The next day, baby Mark and I were in the grocery store. Mr. and Mrs. Carpenter were also in the store. They spoke and expressed how happy they were to have the Smith family in the church parsonage. They commented about how much they enjoyed Joe's first sermon. I graciously thanked them.

Then I continued shopping. Mark needed baby food, and I needed more cleaning supplies. Soon, at the checkout counter, I was unloading the buggy, and in my buggy was a can of snuff!

Laying the can aside, I said to the checkout lady, "I didn't put this in my buggy. Someone is trying to pull a little joke on me."

Of course, I knew Mr. Carpenter was guilty of slipping the snuff in the buggy. I saw him down an aisle, watching and chuckling. Shaking my head, I gave him a "you naughty guy" smile. It was obvious that he was enjoying his practical joke on a prissy, young lady from Georgia.

Mark was about fourteen months old when he found a visiting relative's bottle of allergy pills. They were colorful pills, and I'm sure looked like candy to him. The little climber got himself on a chair and reached them in the middle of the table. He had a couple of the pills swallowed before I could take away the medicine. This was a frightening experience!

Joe was gone with our only car, so I ran down the sidewalk, with my baby in my arms, looking for a neighbor at home with a car. My next-door neighbors were all gone, working or shopping. I saw a car in a carport several houses away. I ran there and urgently knocked on the door. A man answered. I quickly explained that I needed to take my baby to the emergency room. "Let me grab my keys, and we'll be on the way!" he said.

It was enough to ask for a ride from a stranger, but on the way to the hospital, he began telling how we had saved his life by ringing the doorbell. At the moment I rang their doorbell, he and his wife were arguing.

He said, "She put down the gun when the doorbell rang. Hearing the problem about your baby changed her mind about shooting me."

I was so thankful to get to the emergency room door. The man asked, "Do I need to wait?"

I said, "No, thanks, I'll call my husband."

Soon, the doctor was working on my baby, trying to suction out his stomach. That wasn't working well; the tube kept getting stopped up, and my baby was screaming!

I told the nurse and doctor that I had just given Mark sliced grapes for a snack before he found the pills. That was stopping up the suction tube.

With that information, they decided to give him something to make him throw up. And he did! They said the grapes had absorbed the harmful pills and were helpful in bringing them out as well.

The doctor made a hurtful remark during his frustration with the suction process not working. He said, "Some people shouldn't have children, and this is an example why."

I knew I was a good mother, so that statement was a bad one, and I felt insulted. I was young, only twenty-two, but I loved my baby and never wanted him to have such an accident. The remark hurt my already tender emotions. We never used that doctor again.

When Joe finally got to the hospital, I broke down in sobs. It had been a very, very dramatic morning. But we were thankful that our baby was okay.

Down the street from the parsonage, I never heard about anyone being shot, so I guess the man's life was saved too.

It wasn't long after President Kennedy visited the Homestead airbase that we experienced the Cuban Missile Crisis.

It was during the last few months of 1962 that we knew there were reports of evidence of Soviet offensive missile sites being set up in Cuba and that they were a danger to the United States. President Kennedy had said in a speech, "It shall be policy of this nation to regard any nuclear missile launched from Cuba as an attack by the Soviet Union on the United States, requiring a full retaliatory response upon the Soviet Union."

By January 1963, the Homestead airbase was still on a round-the-clock high alert. Every few minutes, there was the sound of another fighter jet leaving the base, getting ready to protect South Florida.

Overnight, the farmers' fields were filled with newly set up army tents. With soldiers and their equipment all over the place, Homestead looked like a war zone. This made the citizens nervous, so people were leaving Homestead by the hundreds. They were going up North to be with relatives and friends.

I was expecting my second baby in a couple of weeks. My new doctor advised me not to take the long ride back to Georgia. Because of some complications, it was recommended that I stay off my feet and in bed most of the time during my last few weeks.

Like a captain with a sinking ship, Joe was caring for his church members, a pregnant wife, and a sixteen-month-old Mark.

One family in the Redlands was preparing to leave Homestead because of the war threat. Joe went to bid them goodbye. He found them butchering the family's pet pig. He came home laughing and told me the story.

"I swear they had actually killed that pet pig and were trying to clean it with just cups of hot water and a razor blade. They planned to pack it on ice and take it all the way up to Pennsylvania. I remembered how Grandpapa cleaned and butchered hogs on his farm in Georgia, and I said, 'Man, that's not the way to clean a hog! A Cuban missile could hit before you finish cleaning a hog that way. Get some buckets of boiling water to pour over the hog. That should make the job a little easier and faster.' Of course, he didn't have the equipment to do it like on Granddaddy's farm. I just had to leave before I cried with the children or laughed at the man."

That funny story, along with all the tensions of a war alert, sent me into labor. About midnight, baby Luke was born in the Homestead hospital.

He was the first Florida Cracker in the Smith family.

But I didn't have to worry about Luke catching pneumonia. Mark's birth had been maddening with so many visitors. This time there were only a few people visiting and kissing baby Luke. Everyone was busy with the threat of war on their doorsteps. Soon, the Soviets backed down and agreed to remove missiles from Cuba if the United States would lift the blockade and guarantee no invasion. Thank God, our lives could get back to a more normal pace.

When Luke was six weeks old, I took him to the church for his baptism. It was well done by Daddy Joe. He received lots of oohs and coos about his thick black hair, big hazel eyes, and fat cheeks. He was a beautiful, healthy baby!

To have babies only seventeen months apart was a lot of work for a young mother. But Joe and I were thankful and proud of our healthy little boys.

By the time Luke was over a year old, he and his brother, Mark, looked just alike. I dressed them identically and enjoyed having strangers ask if they were twins.

While my babies took their afternoon naps, I took college courses, one at a time. I took these courses through the University of Florida Extension Home Study Program. The courses included child psychology, nutrition, and literature. Each course helped me work toward my goal of earning a degree. With family and church meetings that I was expected, as the minister's wife, to attend, I did not have the time, energy, or the extra funds to go to school full-time.

I was a very protective mother and always put my babies first. With so many working moms, I felt blessed that I could be home with my children. We had social occasions with other stay-at-home mothers. My children were happy, and so was I.

When Mary Alice Jones, a successful children's author, was visiting and speaking at churches in the Homestead and Miami areas, she accepted a dinner invitation and visited us at our parsonage. She was impressed that Mark and Luke already had two of her books, *My First Book About God* and *My First Book About Jesus*. When she returned home, she sent them a whole box of her children's books! We were impressed. It was such a thoughtful gift.

There was an older businessman and a thirty-two-year-old young divorcée with a Marilyn-Monroe look in the Redland Community Methodist Church choir. The businessman was impressed, and he hired her as his secretary. Sure, she was a desperate housewife needing a job, but she became more than a secretary for her boss. That got her and him in a lot of trouble when the man's wife, Tiny, realized what was going on.

Tiny walked into her family's business office one Monday morning, took off her high-heeled shoe, and gave the secretary a beating! A black-and-blue secretary left the office. And a guilty husband was afraid to go home. He was a desperate husband with a very angry wife, and he needed his minister's advice.

Joe said, "I had to practice my book-learned psychology on Mr. Thomas." At this early stage in his ministry, Joe didn't have much experience counseling guilty, sin-sick husbands.

Of course, Preacher Joe also lost his best soprano in the church choir. She was too embarrassed to return to the Redland church.

I was amused with the whole story; and with a twinkle in my eye, I teased Joe, saying, "Just let that be a lesson to you about hanky-panky relationships with good-looking choir members. I now know what high-heeled shoes are good for."

While in Homestead, I was given the custody of another sister, Evelyn. I brought her home from a hospital in Georgia after she almost died from a ruptured appendix. I nursed her back to health. Then she was able to join Lois at the Methodist boarding school in Thomasville, Georgia. I had graduated from the same school before going to the nursing school in Moultrie. I knew the Vashti teachers and housemothers had good discipline and teaching methods, and my sisters would have training in manners and morals as well as in the academics.

I now had responsibility for two sisters as well as my two young sons. Joe was very supportive. I still wondered if I was strong enough to meet the challenge.

It helped a lot when Joe said, "You know, someday when we grow old, we may look back on our lives and see that the best thing we ever did was take care of your sisters. We share our home with them, and they share their love for our children."

In the summers, as Joe and I attended conferences and meetings, Lois and Evelyn babysat and spoiled Mark and Luke. They had breaks from the boarding school during summers and holidays. This gave me a chance to join Joe with some of the extra church work. Lois played games with the boys, and Evelyn baked lots of sugar cookies. To their nephews, they were more like big sisters than aunts.

Next door to the Homestead parsonage lived two middle-aged working women with a big, mean dog. He looked like a German shepherd, but the women said he was a wolf and German shepherd mix. They kept telling us neighbors, "He's a good dog, very loyal, and we love him."

They may have loved their dog, but the neighbors didn't love that dog. The dog was in a fenced-off backyard that joined the parsonage backyard. While his masters were working, he kept getting out of the gate. It had a weak latch.

One day, he got out and attacked a grandfather as he was pushing his grandchild around the block in a stroller. The man screamed for help as the mean dog bit his legs! A good neighbor came to his rescue with a bamboo stick.

One Saturday morning, the dog got out while his masters were home.

This mean dog ran across our front yard as he saw the neighbors getting out of their car on the other side of the parsonage. He was going for the neighbor's pregnant wife!

The young woman's husband was an air force pilot, assertive and strong. As his heavy boots hit the sidewalk toward the dog, the mean dog seemed to feel his anger. The dog stuck his tail under his body as he turned around and ran for his own yard. His master stood in her yard, calling him back.

"Lady, if you ever let that dog out of your yard again and I catch him, I'll kill him with my bare hands." He was one angry, upset father-to-be, ready to protect his wife and his unborn child.

Apparently, the woman did not understand that her neighbors meant business. The next week, I was sweeping my front driveway when the dog came across the yard, growling toward my toddler Mark as he was riding his tricycle on the sidewalk. I ran and chased the mean animal with my broom. The dog ran back to his own yard as I hit him with the broom.

As soon as I got my child safely inside the house, I called animal control. Shortly afterward, the dog was picked up and taken to the pound.

That evening, the dog's owner came knocking on the parsonage door, complaining, "I had to pay a big fine to get my dog out of the pound!"

She never apologized about her dog's behavior, and I wasn't impressed with her attitude or her dog. "If he gets out of your yard, I will not hesitate to call the dogcatcher again. Besides, if he bites someone or harms a child, you will be sued."

Something I said must have worked because the women fixed the gate's weak latch, and the mean dog was never seen out of his backyard again.

The women and their mean dog moved, and the house was sold to another air force family. Now my children had nice playmates next door instead of a mean dog.

It was a warm November day as usual in Homestead, Florida, when the airbase neighbor called out across the parsonage backyard. "Have you heard the news? The president has been shot!"

I was watching the children play on their swing set, and Joe had just gotten home for lunch. He had joined us in the backyard when the neighbor told us the shocking news. Taking the boys inside for lunch, we turned on the television, and the sad news was on.

It was November 22, 1963, and the president of the United States had been assassinated by a gunman in Dallas, Texas. The news reports as well as the funeral service were on television for days. President Kennedy's style and quick wit had endeared him to the American people. Also, his beautiful wife and lovely children gave the White House a wonderful family image. This was all destroyed in an instant, and the American people grieved. We even saw the assassin, Lee Harvey Oswald, shot as the police moved him from a car to a jail. Such real-life drama on television was shocking!

After the president's assassination, life got back on schedule with daily living and work as usual. Joe's new project was remodeling the church sanctuary. The contractor spirit in Joe saw how the church needed some interior work that would make it more worshipful and attractive for the congregation. He pointed this out to the board members, and they agreed. Joe enjoyed overseeing his first church remodeling project.

A couple of years went by in Homestead. Then the bishop told Joe's district superintendent to inform the Redland church that their young pastor was needed in another church. The bishop would send the Redland church a new pastor. The people had hoped Joe could stay longer. Not only had he improved the looks of the church, but the attendance and membership had grown. With mixed feelings about moving, we packed up our personal belongings.

FRUITLAND PARK COMMUNITY UNITED METHODIST CHURCH: 1965-1968

U NDER A PICTURE of our family, the Leesburg newspaper printed these words: "The Fruitland Park Methodist Church gets a new pastor, Rev. Joe Hudson Smith, wife Gloria and two sons, Mark and Luke."

In the sixties, Fruitland Park was still a sleepy little community, very slow paced with beautiful, moss-covered oak trees. It was a village of homes, schools, and churches. Some of the homes were on a lake. It had a quick market and a few businesses. Most of the people worked in the surrounding areas of Leesburg and Clermont. There was talk that a large Disney World was soon going to be built in Orlando, and that would bring much growth to the area. At this time, it was mostly orange groves between Fruitland Park and Orlando.

The members of the Fruitland Park church had just finished building a new sanctuary. It was very modern with a high praying-hands pitched roof, large beams showing inside, and large floor-to-ceiling glass down the sides. The sanctuary was beautiful! They also had a new fellowship hall and Sunday school rooms.

The Fruitland Park members were not wealthy. Not enough money had been raised before building the new church plant. Now, one doctor, a ranch owner, and a few businessmen were giving extra, trying to meet the monthly budget. Joe spent a lot of his time raising money to pay the bills, along with his pastoral duties.

Several blocks away sat the old church building, so Joe advised the board, "Let's sell that property." They sold the old church building to another denomination. Selling the old church helped pay down some of the debt on the new church.

The Fruitland Park community needed a kindergarten. This was before kindergarten programs had been added to the public schools in the area. I wanted to organize a much-needed school for five-year-olds. I didn't want to drive to Leesburg for my children's kindergarten. And I learned that other parents didn't like having to find a school outside the community for their children. The church board agreed to sponsor the kindergarten program, and we used the new fellowship hall and Sunday school rooms for our school.

Mark was ready for kindergarten. My friend Boots had a young son ready for kindergarten too. Since she was an experienced first-grade teacher, I asked her to help me organize and teach the kindergarten. We made a good team. Our program included academics, arts, music, and games. Three-year-old Luke joined us at the kindergarten and did a good job keeping up with the older children. Few children get to go to kindergarten three years before they are old enough for first grade. Luke had a lot of preschool experience, so he grew up fast, keeping up with older children as well as his older brother at home.

Boots and I took the children on interesting field trips. Often the trips were reported in the Leesburg newspaper with a picture of the kindergarteners. Parents loved seeing their children in the news. There were trips to see farms the local jail, and there were train rides to Silver Springs in Ocala. Our kindergarten was a success, and it met the needs of children in the Fruitland Park community.

Two nights a week, I attended the local community college, taking courses in literature, science, and history. Many of the night students were young adults, so I felt comfortable in the classes.

My sister Lois was a day student at the college, so she was home with the boys when I was in class. Joe usually had a night meeting.

I was still in my twenties when I was asked by another judge to make decisions concerning my baby sister and brothers. With an alcoholic father and a sick mother, the children needed to be taken out of foster homes. Could I find homes for them with friends or relatives? I already had the responsibility of my sisters, Lois and Evelyn, and I wasn't financially able to care for the others. But I could keep them together by finding placements for them.

At that time, the children were spending summer vacation with us from their foster home in Georgia. With my younger siblings in all the parsonage beds, as well as on the sofa and in sleeping bags on the living room floor, I watched over my sleeping brothers and sisters as a Florida storm raged outside. The creepy moss was flying against the windows from the large oaks in the yard.

I prayed, "God, please keep my family safe. And help me make the right decisions for my brothers' and sisters' future." I silently wondered if I could stand strong in my personal storm as the giant oaks had stood for years in the many Florida storms.

With the cooperation of the Georgia judge and social services, Joe and I found homes for my siblings. Two brothers, Wayne and Larry, were adopted by friends in Homestead. My little eight-year-old brother, David, and my baby sister, Toni, were adopted by the Galbreaths in Fruitland Park. They lived on a ranch with horses and cows. Mike, a brother in college, was part of a doctor's family in Georgia. Wilbur, our oldest brother, was working and living on his own.

The story of how I managed family problems and how I rescued my brothers and sisters from a dysfunctional family life would fill another book.

As the oldest of nine, I always knew I would be the one to take responsibility for my brothers and sisters. And until I met Joe, I was planning to do it alone. He convinced me that it was too big a job for me to do by myself. He said, "With God's help, we can do it together." And we did! Together, we could climb every mountain.

In the summers, Joe and I took our sons and my sisters on camping trips to places like Ocala National Forest, Jekyll Island campground, and the Florida beaches. Living in Florida gave us lots of opportunities for fun and recreation. With tents and a camper, we had a lot of miserable fun in the North Carolina Mountains. It always seemed to rain in those mountains. The tents got wet, which meant the children had to pile in the camper. We did have nice days too, and we enjoyed taking day trips near our campsites.

We also visited relatives in Georgia. Joe's parents continued to live in Moultrie, so that town became holy ground for Mark and Luke. They were the only grandchildren, and they got a lot of spoiling. Grandmother Grace called it good spoiling. We agreed that extra attention and love is good for children.

We were excited about the grandparents buying a farm. It had some fishponds, a camp house, and a barn. The boys looked forward to visiting the Georgia farm where Joe, Mark, and Luke enjoyed fishing and hunting with Granddaddy Hubert. The grandparents kept their home in town, but they often spent weekends at the farm. There were horses to ride, cows to feed, and other animals to enjoy. It was a great place to entertain relatives and friends!

A minister and his family are not exempt from the sorrows and problems of life. Joe's parents had adopted his sister, Fran, when she was four years old. Now she was dead at the age of twenty. After finishing a year of college at the University of Georgia, Fran decided to take a year off to work as a reporter. She was already a gifted writer, and her future looked bright. On a cold, rainy day in Georgia, Fran was buried in Moultrie. That was a sad day for the Smith family.

Fran's birth mother had abandoned her and her three-year-old sister, leaving them with relatives and an alcoholic father living nearby. Fran's birth father was a distant cousin of Joe's mother. Joe's parents adopted Fran with the birth father's blessings. Another relative adopted Fran's sister. The sisters grew up in the same neighborhood, so they were together a lot as they grew up.

Fran became deeply depressed after a bad experience happened to her. She was working late one night on an accident call for her reporter job. Before getting back to her apartment, two black guys caught her, forced her at gunpoint into a car, took her to the woods, and raped her. They left her for dead after she was badly beaten up. Naked and barely able to move, she made it to a farmhouse, got help, and was taken to the hospital. Fran had convinced her close friend and the authorities not to call her parents. She went to court all by herself and watched the criminals found guilty, and they were later sent to prison. Hearing this horrible experience that Fran went through all by herself without her family's help was extra devastating to her family.

Fran had always been the quiet type, and even at family gatherings, she would sometimes go off in a corner of a room and read a book while everyone was visiting and socializing.

While working on the university school paper, Fran met a young man named Louis Gizzard. A few months before her death, Fran told Joe that she wanted him to meet her new friend. She said, "You'll like him, Joe! He acts and talks a lot like you." Fran wasn't the type to gush over young men, but we thought she must be fond of him since she wanted us to meet him. Later, Gizzard became a popular Southern writer, and one night, Joe was reading one of his books and found that he was mentioning Fran's untimely death. He wrote how he thought she had been one of the most promising young writers that he had ever met. Maybe their friendship had been more special than we had known since he also grieved her death.

Fran was an attractive, smart girl, and Joe's parents had showered her with lots of love. Sometimes, a bad experience can overpower love.

The next Sunday, after the funeral, Joe shared his grief with his congregation. As his chin quivered, he said, "Depression and some bad experiences caused my sister, Fran, to take her own life. My family and I thank you for your thoughts and prayers during this sad time for our family."

A few weeks later, along with Joe's parents, we bought and placed a beautiful fountain in a garden between the Fruitland Park church sanctuary and the fellowship hall. Memorials were given in her memory at our church as well as the First United Methodist Church in Moultrie. We would always keep her precious memory in our hearts.

Mark started first grade in the little elementary school across the street from the parsonage. Daddy Joe walked his son across the street that first school day as I watched from the living room window, tears rolling down my cheeks. My firstborn was going out into the great big world! I would no longer be the center of his young life. Kindergarten was over. There would be other teachers, peers, and books.

After school, the street in front of the parsonage was busy with parents picking up their children, school buses leaving the school, and children walking everywhere. Joe excused himself from a guest as he went to help Mark safely cross the street. A proud little future lawyer walked beside his dad with his book pack and snack box in hand.

"Mark, how was your first day of school?"

"Well, I tell you, Dad, it was damn hot!"

Daddy Joe just secretly smiled and showed no alarm over his son's newly acquired vocabulary.

It was August. Without air-conditioning in his classroom, it must have been quite miserable. The teacher had promised that the problem would be fixed, and they would have a cool room by the next day.

Joe couldn't wait to tell what Mark had learned on his first day of school. He knew Pete and Jane would be amused. Pete was also a Methodist minister. *He would be shocked*, he thought. But it was too good not to tell, and Joe loved telling a good story. Reverend Pete and Jane were greatly amused and laughed forever; it seemed to me as I sat there, surprised and speechless.

Pete said, "Son like father."

Joe said, "No, son like mother."

Thank goodness Mark had gone to his room and missed all the amusement about his first day of school. After a hug from his mother, his brother, Luke, had cheerfully welcomed him home. They had spirited games to play! Putting on their Superman outfits, they ran outside.

"Joe, I keep seeing Mr. Blair [husband and grandfather] and Ms. Dixie [widow] working quite often in the church's flower garden. I think something more than flowers is blooming there."

They were sixty-five or older, but to a young minister's wife, they looked too old to be acting like teenagers. Surely, they shouldn't be having a romantic interest in each other, I thought.

"Oh, Gloria, they're just good friends, and they're doing a good job cleaning the flower beds and cutting the hedges around the church." Joe hadn't paid much attention to their actions.

"Well, why would good friends affectionately touch each other as they meet in the church parking lot?"

"Gloria, are you sure you're seeing that well all the way across the empty field?"

"Joe, I have a bird's-eye view from my kitchen window, and I have twenty-twenty vision," I reminded him.

A few weeks later, Mrs. Blair visited Joe at the church office, complaining that her husband was neglecting his family. She said, "He comes home late in the evenings, skips meals at home, and ignores his grandson."

I nodded, "Maybe he's spending time in the flower garden at Ms. Dixie's house?"

A couple of years later, Mr. Blair divorced his wife and married Ms. Dixie at the courthouse. After that, the Methodist Church's flower garden was neglected because Mr. Blair and Ms. Dixie went to the Baptist Church.

Someone made light of the situation, saying that Mrs. Blair lost a husband, and the church lost some unfaithful garden keepers. Mrs. Blair now cries and sings, "I come to the garden alone while teardrops fall on the roses."

On a more serious note, ministers see the hurt caused by divorce. People's deepest emotions are injured when love is lost and families are broken. Of course, there are situations where divorce is best, but a lot of marriages might be saved if people were more loyal and remembered their wedding vows. Some people act like cows, thinking it is just greener on the other side of the fence.

Most of the faithful members at the Fruitland Park Methodist church stood strong, and many good people lead the future forward.

Great-granddaddy Hudson and Great-grandmother Eella came for a visit to Fruitland Park. Joe was lucky to have them visit each of his new appointments before they died. I felt Mark and Luke were lucky to have grandparents and extra blessed to know their great-grandparents. We knew the great-grandparents' visit was special because they didn't travel very much anymore. We usually saw them at their home and farm in Funston, a little farm village near Moultrie, Georgia. It was amazing that they had never spent the night apart in more than fifty years of marriage.

Standing on the parsonage front steps, Granddaddy Hudson was taking in the scene of the schoolyard across the street. There were little black and white children holding hands, running and playing together on the school grounds. Integration was a new and different scene for Joe's grandfather. He knew that it wasn't coming about without a lot of stress and uprising on the streets all over the South.

How did a minister and his wife handle the negative views of some of the people around them?

Our acceptance of all people no matter their color had to be handled with care to keep from stirring up negative reactions. Some of our minister friends in Georgia had gone to jail during sit-ins and marches. We quietly set an example of Christian love, teaching little children to sing songs like "Jesus loves all the children of the world, red, and yellow, black and white; they are all precious in his sight." Joe also preached sermons on caring for others no matter the color of their skin or their nationality.

"MARTIN LUTHER KING SHOT" was the headline in the paper.

It was April 4, 1968, when he was shot dead in Memphis, Tennessee, where he was to lead a march of sanitation workers protesting against low wages and poor working conditions. Martin Luther King Jr. was a prominent American civil rights leader, and he had advocated the use of nonviolent tactics when he led marches and sit-ins.

People were concerned about the future of the country with so many assassinations over the last few years. First, it was President Kennedy, then his brother Robert, and now Martin Luther King Jr.

A lot of people still had negative feelings about integration. More people needed to show love and forgiveness instead of fear and hate. Human progress is sometimes slow. But we had faith that better days would come, when more people would have true freedom and the American dream. Maybe a more peaceful world could be possible if only people would realize that love and understanding are greater than hate and ignorance.

Joe's district superintendent called. "Joe, the bishop is appointing you to another church in June. The bishop's cabinet thinks you deserve a salary increase. Three years of hard work without much of a raise because of the church's debt isn't fair to you and your family. You will be appointed to the Keystone United Methodist Church in Odessa."

"Odessa?" Joe asked. "Where is that?"

"It's located near Tampa," the superintendent informed Joe.

After getting the message, Joe decided we should ride over to Odessa. It was a few weeks before moving date, but curiosity took over. What does the place look like?

What a culture shock! Odessa was just a post office and an ugly junkyard! There was nothing else in sight except scrub oaks and grass. Our first impression of Odessa wasn't a positive one.

From the post office, we drove through several more miles of isolated countryside; then, we passed a little country village shopping center and went down another country road before reaching the church. I now had tears running down my cheeks. We stopped in the church parking lot, got out of the car, and walked around the church grounds. There was disappointment on Joe's face.

It was an old sanctuary, sitting beside a cemetery. A marker said it was established in 1868. The present building had been erected about 1914. It was now 1968.

Joe tried to be positive; with a crying wife and serious-looking sons, he said, "Well, it looks like there may be some progressive folks here because they have a new and neat fellowship hall."

"But it's not as nice as the country churches we had in Georgia. At least, they had air-conditioning." I commented.

The church plant had a peaceful country setting, with no homes or even a town in sight. On the road by the church was a sign pointing to the Tampa horse-racing track.

"Can we go to the horse races?" Luke humorously asked, trying to cheer everyone up a bit.

It was hard not to judge this place by first appearances. We would have to reach down deep within and find our dedication. We were in the ministry to love and serve people. But where were the people? In June, on the next moving date, we would find out.

KEYSTONE UNITED METHODIST CHURCH: 1968-1973

T HE KEYSTONE UNITED Methodist Church is located on Race Track Road near Tampa, Florida.

In the sixties and early seventies, Keystone was a countrylike bedroom community, several miles outside the city. Keystone was a community hidden down private lanes and country roads, with beautiful lakes and nice, average homes. The people were families who had lived in the area for a long time. Some were professionals who wanted to live on a lake outside the city. Many lived on Lake Keystone, which had homes all around it. There were several smaller lakes with homes around them too.

The Methodist parsonage was located by one of the smaller lakes. It was a perfect location for two little boys to enjoy fishing and swimming.

Soon after arriving in Keystone, I was busy helping my sister Lois with wedding plans. She was engaged to Doug Duston, a bright engineering student at the University of Florida. Lois was still a member of the Fruitland Park church, so she wanted Joe to give the vows for her and Doug. At first, Joe felt uncomfortable about going back so soon to a former church to perform the wedding.

The new minister at the Fruitland Park church understood why Lois needed her brother-in-law to perform her wedding. He called Joe, and the wedding date was set.

When ministers move, the parsonage children still have friends in the former church where they grew up who are graduating from high school or college. So that is where they usually decide to have their weddings.

Lois and Doug had a lovely wedding in the beautiful sanctuary at Fruitland Park, surrounded by family and friends. Joe performed the ceremony.

With Joe's help, the church board hired a new sexton. Mr. Brammer needed something useful to do after retirement, so he took the job. He felt this job would keep him active while helping the church. He was a faithful member, and he loved his church. At first, Mr. Brammer was a serious acting fellow around the church. He didn't mean to get humorous, but with his pastor's friendship, they became a fun-loving team.

Joe used Mr. Brammer's weekly comical situations to lighten the mood just before his sermon on Sunday mornings. The people looked forward to the tidbit news stories and were disappointed if Joe didn't have a little community humor each Sunday. Mr. Brammer was a really good sport, always laughing at himself along with the congregation.

Someone gave Joe a motorized toy horse for the church nursery. Joe said, "Mr. Brammer, get on this horse, and let's see if it's safe for the young children to ride."

"Sure, Preacher. If I can ride it, old as I am, any child can. Looks like fun to me!"

Joe turned on the motor. The horse jerked up and down a couple of times and went faster and faster, galloping like a horse out of control. Mr. Brammer yelled, "Stop this darn thing, Joe."

Joe left the motor on a little longer, giving Mr. Brammer the joyride of his life! When Mr. Brammer threatened his pastor's life with a few choice words that couldn't be repeated in church, Joe turned off the motor.

After climbing off the toy horse, Mr. Brammer and his pastor had a good laugh. How could anyone think such a toy was a good idea for young children? They detached the motor. Now, feeling like *heroes*, they just knew they were saving the church from some parent suing them over a hurt child.

Later, the horse was enjoyed by all the nursery and kindergarten children but without a motor. And the congregation had another funny Mr. Brammer story to tell.

The Keystone church parsonage was on a small lake with a very private beach. I loved sunbathing on the beach. We all loved to swim, and Mark and Luke spent hours fishing off the dock. We had only one nearby neighbor. Dr. Swainbom, a retired dentist, who lived in a little cottage next door. He had a large orange grove that covered a few acres from his house to the paved road. From the paved road, we had an unpaved lane that came past his house, and our parsonage was at the end of the lane. With no other neighbors on that side of the lake, we thought we had the most private parsonage in all the state of Florida.

One day, I walked down to the beach with Sheba, our graceful German shepherd. I had been cleaning house all morning, getting ready for a church social in a few days. Now I needed a little rest before the children came home from school. Also, my Cub Scout troupe meeting was later that afternoon. Sunbathing was my favorite way to relax.

While half asleep, I heard a helicopter over the lake, flying low and circling right over me. The men waved as they flew over. What were they up to? I covered myself with a towel. Still, they circled over the lake and flew back over me.

I decided to break up this little joyride! I waved goodbye to the flyers as I walked across the backyard and safely back into the parsonage. They had messed up my resting time.

As soon as I got in the house, the phone rang. It was Joe. "Honey, were you sunbathing nude by the lake? A deputy sheriff just called me at the church office and said, 'Tell your wife to get some clothes on before we wreck our helicopter!'"

"Are you kidding?"

"No, I'm not kidding, but don't worry. It was just one of our church members, the deputy sheriff, and he seemed to find it amusing to catch the minister's wife sunbathing in a bikini!"

That day I discovered that our beach wasn't as private as I had thought. But wearing a bikini was my style, and I had just been myself, not trying to protect the image of a preacher's wife.

It wasn't long before our boys had many friends their age in the community. Of course, their friends' parents became some of our closest friends too. One couple had seven boys, and when some of the boys came over to play with Mark and Luke, they had a whole softball team, which provided hours of fun. The McGill boys went to a Catholic church, but I thought it was good for my children to learn to accept friends from different religious faiths. The little boys' mother, Meg, and I were very good friends, having lots of parenting discussions while our little boys played.

One day, Meg came over with the boys, and her eyes were red from crying. She looked like a death had happened in the family.

"Oh, Meg, What's wrong?" I asked.

"The debt collectors just came and picked up my washing machine. My husband said it will probably be the house next."

Meg's husband was an engineer who had had a good job in Tampa with a large firm, but he had quit that job to try having his own business. Like a lot of young men, he wanted to be his own boss and try his luck at making his own fortune in the world. He was a man of ingenuity, talents, and ambition. Some business ventures make it, and some don't. Meg's husband had borrowed too much money, and now he was losing not only the business, but his family's home as well.

"Meg, you don't have to go all the way into Tampa for a washer. You're welcome to use my washing machine when you need it." It must have been little comfort to a young mother who was losing her home.

It was heavy on my heart knowing it would soon be Christmas, and my sons' dear friends would not have any gifts under their tree. The family had to move way out in the country to a double-wide mobile home.

Meg's spirits were positive in spite of the problems. "We may not have much for Christmas this year, but God has blessed us with Greg getting a job, and we have a roof over our heads, and my boys are healthy."

I shared with friends the story of a family having financial problems with seven boys and no extra money for Christmas without mentioning their names. A dentist gave two hundred dollars, and another family gave another three hundred dollars. We mailed a casher's check to the family without mentioning who it was from. I didn't want Meg to know that we had collected the money. They had had enough embarrassment with losing their home and the standard of living they were use to, so I didn't want them to know who gave the Christmas gift.

When Meg called all excited about receiving an anonymous gift in the mail and how she would be able to buy the boys a good Christmas after all, it was hard not to admit my actions, especially when she said, "Gloria, it had to be someone with a good heart like you and Joe."

Keeping the secret, I said, "Meg, I just prayed that your family would have a good Christmas, and I'm so happy someone was able to share with you."

Circumstances and time can distance friendships, and our boys couldn't play together as often since they moved several miles away, but we continued our friendship until they moved further away.

I would never forget Meg's strong faith as she struggled through losing her nice home and how she quickly became positive in accepting what she could not control. Her faith reminded me of the Serenity Prayer:

> God, grant me the Serenity to accept the things I cannot change
> The courage to change the things I can
> And the Wisdom to know the difference.

One day, Joe was in the middle of writing a sermon at the church office when his phone rang. It was Mrs. Brammer. She seemed very anxious and excited about something.

"Preacher Joe, tell my husband to stop what he is doing and come home right away!"

"He isn't here, Mrs. Brammer. He's gone shopping for cleaning supplies. Are you sick, Mrs. Brammer?"

"No, but there's a monkey trying to break my window! He wants to get into my house."

"Are you sure, Mrs. Brammer? That's probably just Mr. Brammer trying to get you to unlock the door. You know, he does like to monkey around."

"Joe, I'm serious. It's a real monkey! He's banging on my kitchen window and I'm afraid. Help! He's about to break in!"

"Just hold on, Mrs. Brammer. I'm on my way!"

Sure enough, Joe found a hungry, mean-acting monkey trying to break the Brammer's kitchen window. Joe was just about as afraid of the mad monkey as Mrs. Brammer was.

"Give me a banana, Mrs. Brammer. I think he's hungry."

Joe tried giving the monkey the banana, but he refused it. "I don't like bananas, you nut," the monkey seemed to be saying. Then Joe offered him an apple.

"Oh, Lord, the monkey is coming for it!" Joe yelled.

Joe threw the apple in the pump house, and the monkey ran in for it. Quickly, Joe closed the door.

At that moment, Joe became Mrs. Brammer's hero. He had locked the monkey in Mr. Brammer's pump house. Now he needed to find the owner of a runaway monkey. Going around the very large Keystone Lake, he stopped at each house and asked if someone had lost a pet monkey. Finally, the owners were found.

The next Sunday morning, the congregation had a good, long laugh! Joe told them the monkey story and how he first thought it was just Mr. Brammer, acting like a monkey, trying to get in his wife's kitchen window.

After a couple of years at Keystone, Joe came home very excited from a board meeting. He had some good news.

"The board members voted to build a new sanctuary! The contractor told them that the church's beams are not strong enough to risk putting in an air-conditioning system. He also told them that even a strong wind could be dangerous if people were in the building during a storm. Of course, we had one or two who thought we should just leave things as they are. But most of the board members want to build a new sanctuary."

I was so glad they voted to build. Most people in Florida are used to air-conditioning in their homes, and they're not comfortable coming to a church without it. I was happy and excited that we would soon have a new sanctuary.

While Joe was busy with the construction of the new church sanctuary, I was taking more college courses at the St. Petersburg Community College. After getting an associate arts degree, I began substituting for teachers at nearby schools, especially at Mark and Luke's Citrus Park Elementary School. I was so flattered when the principal wanted to hire me full-time. After she found out that I didn't have a bachelor's degree, she said, "Well, you're a natural. Hurry and get your degree finished, so you can teach."

I finished my associate degree in my twenties.

It was like growing up the same time as my children.

Still, it was my goal to get my bachelor's degree. I wanted my children and future grandchildren to know that a college degree was important. Also, I had always felt the little steps following me, with my eight younger sisters and brothers.

Joe liked to get up early on Sunday mornings, about four or five o'clock so he could go to his office and go over his sermon. Sometimes he even practiced it to the empty pews before coming back home for breakfast.

This morning, he was up early as usual, looking around in his closet, and he disturbed my sleep by talking out loud, "I can't find my brown dress shoes. Gloria, do you know what happened to them? Did the dog get them?"

Half asleep, I answered, "I don't know. Maybe you left them in the camper."

With bare feet, Joe went through the wet grass looking for his shoes in the camper.

In the meantime, I woke up enough to remember that I had dropped them in my closet when I was bringing things in from the camper. So I quickly got up, took his shoes out of my closet, and stuck them back in his closet. I was thinking, *That'll teach him to search for himself and stop whining to me at four o'clock in the morning!*

When Joe got back to the bedroom, he again complained to me in a frustrated voice, "Well, they weren't in the camper!"

"Are you sure you looked gooood in your closet?"

He looked again in his closet. Of course, he wondered how he could have overlooked them in plain view.

There was not another word out of Joe. I rolled over and went back to sleep with a smile on my face.

That morning, Joe didn't have a Mr. Brammer story, but he thought he had a good wife story. His sermon was about PATIENCE. He thought he had a good illustration from his own life about losing patience this morning when he couldn't find his shoes.

"I even had the nerve to wake up my wife, asking her about my shoes. And the whole time my brown shoes had been in my closet."

As he said all this, he looked out at me as if apologizing for his grumpy early morning behavior.

After church while having dinner at home, I burst out laughing.

"What's so funny?" Joe asked.

"I found your shoes in my closet and put them back in your closet while you were out in the wet backyard looking for them. I think it's funny that you made it a sermon illustration!"

Realizing the joke was on him. Joe didn't mention that story again. And he didn't wake me up at four o'clock in the morning again.

After many months, a beautiful and larger sanctuary was standing where the old church building had sat. Joe was so proud of that building project, and so were the members.

Joe had just finished another beautiful wedding in the new sanctuary. After the wedding, a young bridesmaid was walking to her car with a bundle of clothes in her arms. Joe was walking behind her, going to his car, when he saw she had dropped something. It was a pair of underwear.

Instead of embarrassing her or himself by saying, "Wait, you dropped your panties," he decided to stick them in his pocket.

After he came home and changed from his suit, I was putting the clothes together to take to the cleaners the next day when I discovered the panties. I always cleaned out pockets, forgotten hankies, pennies, and such.

"Joe, what's this? A pair of panties?" Teasing, I said, "Do I need to get out my high-heeled shoes?" It made me think about the choir member and the businessman's wife in Homestead.

"Oh, yeah, I forgot to tell you about that. A bridesmaid dropped them on the way to her car, so I picked them up."

Here's the rest of the sad story. On the phone, Joe was talking with the bridegroom.

The bridegroom told Joe, "Our friend Sandy was in a bad car accident! She was killed on her way to the country club for the reception."

After hanging up the phone, Joe said, "If only I had stopped her and given her the underwear, maybe a delayed second would have made a difference."

I said, "Joe, accidents happen. Even the bride might be saying, 'If only I hadn't set the time of my wedding that late, knowing that winding Gunn Highway is so dangerous after dark.'"

That was a long evening, with Joe visiting the family, trying to answer everyone's questions as well as his own. "God, why do young people have to go this way?" There are no pat answers. The minister and friends show God's love to the family by just being there, holding hands, saying a prayer, and wiping tears together.

One afternoon, Mr. Brammer drove up to the church parking lot and saw cars racing around the circular drive. He jumped out of his car, waving them down while shouting at them, "Don't you have any respect for a church?"

A man with a movie camera walked up to Mr. Brammer's car window, explaining that they had permission from the pastor and the church board to use the parking lot to film part of a movie. "Mister, you've just gotten yourself in the movie!"

"Oh, nobody told me, and I'm the church sexton!"

The next Sunday, Joe had another Mr. Brammer story. "Everyone needs to know that Mr. Brammer is now a movie star!" Then he told how this had happened in the church parking lot. Mr. Brammer blushed and proudly grinned as everyone laughed and clapped.

Some afternoons, after Joe came home from work, Dr. Swainbom, the eighty-nine-year-old neighbor, called across the yard, "Beer time, Joe!" That meant he wanted to talk. He gave Joe a Coke as he drank his beer. He had interesting stories from his own life. Dr. Swainbom had been in three wars – World War I, World War II, and later he was in the Korean conflict.

While Dr. Swainbom was overseas, his wife deserted him and his four children. He then raised his children without a mother. While he was out of the country, he had the help of relatives. Other times, he hired a nanny to care for the children. When he was at home, he cared for them himself.

After his children were grown, Dr. Swainbom retired to Keystone. He lived in the little cottage beside his orange grove. He worked in the grove almost every day. He had little social life. His family lived up North and seldom came to visit. There were never any other visitors, except Joe. He was a strange, quiet man.

Our brother-in-law, Doug, was drafted to Vietnam. He wanted Lois and baby Daniel to be near family while he was gone, so Lois rented an apartment across the lake from the parsonage.

Evelyn had graduated from the Methodist girls school and was going to St. Petersburg Community College. She had a room at the parsonage but spent most nights with Lois and baby Daniel at their apartment across the lake.

One late evening, the boys were still fishing as Evelyn and I sat by the lake, chatting and watching the boys pull in little fish. All of a sudden, we saw a young man running down to the lake. He jumped in the water and was swimming across! He had run from the home of one of the teenage boys who came to the church youth group. I was concerned that he may not make it across the wide lake.

I said, "Evelyn, hurry, take the life preserver in the boat and row out to meet him!"

At first, I couldn't help feeling disgusted that he would do such a foolish thing. He probably just wanted to show off his swimming skills and get our attention. Everyone knew he had a crush on my beautiful sister. I was ready to give him a lecture.

When he got safely to the shore, it was a different story, indeed! He had been beaten and emotionally abused by his stepfather. He had verbally attacked his stepfather about abusing his sister and had threatened to report him to the authorities. Then the angry stepfather hit him with a baseball bat. In his shock, the young man felt he should swim across the lake for his pastor's help.

That night, the young man slept in our camper, safely away from an abusive stepfather. All the right steps were taken to help him and his sister. The family services placed them with an uncle's family.

Years later, when the young man was in the marines, he wrote a thank-you letter to his pastor's family. He remembered how they had come to his rescue when he had that very disturbing experience.

It made us realize that sometimes, dealing with a war in another country cannot be as hurtful to a young person as a family war.

After Evelyn graduated from college, she and Joe's cousin, Cary Hall, became engaged. They wanted to have their wedding in the lovely new sanctuary at Keystone! The whole congregation was invited to the wedding, and Joe performed the ceremony. The Smith and Manning families were present. All of our brothers and sisters and their adopted parents were present too.

Evelyn was a beautiful bride in her white Victorian-style gown.

Mark and Luke and a couple of other ten- and eleven-year-old boys, all cousins, were sitting together in the same pew. Joe was in the middle of the vows when the little boys got tickled. This in turn tickled Granddaddy Hubert, who was trying to keep his amusement hidden. Holding the laughter inside affected his facial expression, making it look as if he were crying. His mother, Joe's grandmother, saw her son looking as if he were crying, and this upset her. She began crying and wiping tears. Toni, the bride's teenage sister, was emotional about her big sister getting married, so she joined in with her sobs.

Later Evelyn said, "When I heard the sobs and giggles, I thought something was wrong with my dress or veil."

Joe ignored the sounds, went on with the ceremony, and wedding memories were made.

Funny things do happen at weddings. Over the years, we witnessed many humorous moments at weddings and wedding receptions. But it is funnier at other people's wedding than when it is at your own.

Just before the wedding, our brother-in-law Doug arrived safely home from Vietnam. He and Lois, along with baby Daniel, moved to Panama City. The parsonage was empty of the laughter of sisters, and the boys missed their doting aunts. My parenting responsibility for my sisters was over. Now, we could act more like sisters instead of me being the parent figure.

A church member gave Joe a boat, and the boys enjoyed skiing on the lake. One afternoon, I decided I would try skiing around the lake. Joe raced the motor at full speed as he tried to pull me up. I was almost up when I felt like I hit a stump. This sudden hard fall shocked me, and I didn't turn loose the rope. Of course, this did the damage. My back would never be the same. In the flash of a second, a healthy young mother would now face years of surgeries and pain. Joe and sons had a hard time without the strong wife and mother they were used to having. I was now very painfully ill. But life would have to go on.

Just before our move from Keystone, Mr. Dan, a Tampa television news commentator, had a piece on the evening news about "a pastor called Joe." He said, "The Keystone Methodist church is grieving. Pastor Joe is moving. The bishop called. Joe and his family will be missed not only by his parish, but he will be missed by the Keystone community. We wish him the best."

We would certainly miss all of our Keystone friends. Our children had played together, and we had shared our lives in so many ways. We would miss the Carithers, the Jacksons, the Hillers, the Giles, the Carnes, the Schoenborns, and so many other dear friends.

Joe and Gloria – 1959 Wedding

Joe and Gloria's Wedding

Reverend Joe – 8 years old going to Sunday School

Gloria – Sweet Sixteen

Gloria and Baby Mark at Kite Parsonage

Joe, Gloria and Baby Mark on their way to Homestead

Joe and Gloria with young sons, Mark and Luke in Homestead, FL.

The Smith Family arrives at Fruitland Park.

Our Beautiful sister Lois – 1967

Smith Family in Keystone – 1971

At Vashti   School '70

Our studious sister Evelyn; Recent Teacher of the Year.

Smith Family in Lake Wales – 1973

Mark and parents at his Law School graduation.

Mark and his bride Martha.

Luke with parents and grandparents and Mark after his
F.S.U. graduation.

Luke and his mom Bride Karen with his mom and dad and Mark
and Martha.

Luke and Karen with young first cousins, served as rice girls for
their wedding.

Gloria hosting another party in Leesburg.

Gloria, the model in stuart.

Gloria, the hostess wherever she goes.

With Humor, Joe and Gloria share Christmas greetings with family
and friends.

Gloria holding a Rose after an inspirational speech for Minister's Mates.

Joe and Gloria's 30th Wedding anniversary in Stuart, Fl.

Joe, the pastor always shaking hands with people as they entered or exited his churches.

Gloria at a Miniature Horse Farm with her little dog, Rambo.

Smith Granddaughter, Whitney with Giang and Kim enjoying the
little horse in Ocala.

Joe and Gloria having fun at retirement party in Gainesvillle.

The smith grandchildren L. to R. Amy, Meredith, Whitney, Claire, Jay
Hudson, David and Katie.

The Smith Family Home for Thanksgiving.

LAKE WALES, FLORIDA: 1973-1981

WHEN THE DISTRICT superintendent called, he said, "Joe, the bishop has appointed you to the First United Methodist Church of Lake Wales."

We knew Lake Wales was a lovely small town. We had been there visiting friends. Tourists visited Lake Wales for the beautiful Bok Tower and the little hill called Spook Hill. People parked their cars on the bottom of the hill and watched their car roll uphill. Of course, the lay of the land was an illusion that made it appear as if the car were rolling uphill when it was actually rolling downhill.

Several miles before reaching Lake Wales, we saw the famous Bok Tower. It was built in the 1920s by Edward Bok, who wanted the world to be a little more beautiful because he had lived in it. Surrounding Bok Tower are beautiful gardens, ponds, large oak trees, and wildlife. It is a lovely sanctuary! Looking down a hill from the tower are mansions that once belonged to the rich and famous. They came to this spot to enjoy warm winter vacations. The Mountain Lake Estates were just cottages for those people. Now they are the homes of the Lake Wales community, and some of the Methodist Church members lived there.

When we moved to Lake Wales, the old downtown area still had a quaint and relaxed feel about it, with special shops and a few gourmet restaurants. As with most towns, the newer shopping areas were in a different location.

The Methodist Church was surrounded by palms and manicured lawns and had a tropical Florida look. In the tall steeple nestled a wonderful bell tower. Its bell rang out on Sunday mornings, and the chimes played in the evenings during the week. The steeple could be viewed from the lake as well as from the tennis courts, the ball field, and the children's play park. The church plant, all in Spanish architecture, included a fellowship hall and a two-story Sunday school building. The stained glass windows were a perfect touch for the sanctuary's additional beauty.

The church and parsonage were within walking distance of a large lake in the center of the community. Lovely homes surrounded the lake.

Joe was humbled and at the same time proud to be appointed to this lovely church and nice community. This was a happy move! There were no feelings of disappointment. Joe and I hoped for such an appointment so our sons could grow up in a small town away from city life. It seemed that our prayers had been answered!

On the front of the First United Methodist Church bulletin on June 10, 1973, was a picture of our family with the following words beneath it:

> Our new minister and family, the Rev. and Mrs. Joe H. Smith, will arrive Thursday, June 14th. Joe and Gloria have two sons, Mark (11) and Luke (10). We welcome them to our Church and to Lake Wales. Throughout the coming years, let us open our hearts to them, and support them with our prayers and faithful service.

The parsonage was located near the church, with an apartment building between it and the church. It was a large house with four bedrooms. A family room as well as a guest room apartment was at the back of the house. This gave some privacy from the street and the football field. There would be some interesting days ahead with a football stadium located across the street from the parsonage.

Joe gave one of his best sermons on that first Sunday in Lake Wales. The people responded with compliments and excitement over having a young pastor's family. It had been several years since the church had a parsonage family with children. The Lake Wales church had been having older senior pastors and young single associate pastors. The members were ready for a family image in the parsonage.

Joe was beaming as he shook hands with each of the people going out the door on that first Sunday. It didn't faze him when one man said, "My wife and I saw you walking downtown yesterday, and we thought the young woman with you was your daughter!"

"No, that was my wife, Gloria." Joe always had people thinking he was much older than his wife.

With a good organist, a talented choir, and a tall young associate, Joe knew he would be challenged to write his best sermons each week. Bill McLoud, the tall associate, and the much shorter Joe made a comical pair going up the aisle side by side like Mutt and Jeff. But Joe always held his head high with short-man confidence. There was no longer a Mr. Brammer to pick on, but Joe now had Bill.

Having two services on Sunday mornings would be a new adjustment for Joe. It was like having two different congregations. This was a larger and more formal church than Joe's past appointments. Of course, we had been members of large First Methodist churches in Georgia when we were teenagers, so we could appreciate having the extras that a larger church supports.

Soon, there was an overflowing, full sanctuary! People were discussing the well-prepared sermons by the Methodist Church's new pastor. When fall arrived, so did the Northern winter visitors. Then chairs had to be placed in the aisles, beside the pews. The side wings filled up. For special services at Easter and Christmas Eve, people came early, trying to get a pew instead of having to sit on a folding chair. Joe's sermons were bringing in the shelves!

The young people's bell choir concerts and the children's musicals filled the church until there was standing room only. Mrs. Stafford was the best children's music director in the state, we thought.

Soon Joe became the community's popular wedding minister. Not only did he have his members' weddings, he had the churched as well as the unchurched. He believed in celebrating married *love*! If the Catholic priest, the Presbyterian minister, or the Baptist minister was too busy or didn't feel a couple met their standards for a wedding in their church, Reverend Joe, the Methodist minister, would be the couple's Parson Smith.

Joe had several weddings at the beautiful Bok Tower. After one of the weddings at the tower, a bridesmaid from Canada stooped down to feed a friendly squirrel. She had on a long knit skirt and accidentally draped it over a red ant bed! She had stooped to give the squirrel a peanut. The bride and groom were busy having their picture taken by the reflection pool. Then, they heard the scream.

"Help! Help! I'm allergic to ants!" As she screamed, she was stepping out of her formal long skirt. Now she was standing in her cute bikini panties as Pastor Joe was trying to wrap his coat around her waist while picking ants off her long, shapely legs.

The tickled photographer was not missing a good snap when she saw one. She couldn't wait to give the snapshot to her minister's wife, laughing and saying, "If you ever need proof of anything, here's a good snapshot!"

In the meantime, Joe took the young woman to our family doctor for an allergy shot. Later, the doctor agreed with Joe that the young woman was very uninhibited when she showed him her ant bites.

The doctor said, "She wasn't shy about pulling down those bikini panties to show me the bites on her backside."

Long after the young woman's pain was relieved and she had left Lake Wales, the story was shared around town. The story was told at the early morning coffee club and at the local Rotary Club. Preacher Joe was praised by his peers for knowing how to save the life of a young bridesmaid in bikini pants from red ants. That story showed how men can have fun with gossip as well as women.

I called Joe at the church office to tell him that I had a call asking for him to go to the local Chinese restaurant. He needed to comfort the owners because their four children, along with their brother, had just been killed in a bad car accident. They had almost gotten home from Disney World when a big truck, loaded with melons, ran into the back of their car as they were turning off busy Highway 60.

I was fighting back tears as I said, "Joe, Mrs. Craig called about the accident, and I could hear the mother screaming in the background. It is a horrible thing to happen to that sweet family."

A few nights before the accident, the young children had helped their parents serve our family dinner at the restaurant. It was a hard funeral for Joe. A couple from another country having to bury all their children was tragic beyond words.

The phone rang after midnight, and I answered it. The caller said, "I want to speak to Joe Smith."

By this time, Joe was wide awake. He thought it must be another emergency or death in the congregation. Late-night calls usually are important.

Taking the phone, he said, "This is Joe."

Then the caller said, "You low-down SOB, this is Mary."

"What's the problem, Mary? Why am I such a low character?"

"I'm pregnant! And you got me pregnant!"

"Mary, I think you have the wrong Joe Smith. I'm the Methodist minister, and this is the Methodist parsonage."

The phone went silent as the caller just hang up.

Amused at such a call, I teased Joe, "What did you mean 'I THINK you have the wrong Joe Smith.' You better KNOW she had the wrong Joe Smith."

A common name like Joe Smith sometimes gets a man in trouble. Joe was taking me out for an anniversary dinner to a nice restaurant at Disney World. When we arrived at the door, the receptionist asked, "Do you have reservations?"

"Yes."

"What's the name?"

"Joe Smith"

"Oh yeah? And she's your secretary." She smiled and nodded toward me.

"No, she's my wife. And it's our anniversary."

"Oh, don't try to explain. It happens here all the time, Joe Smith."

She swiftly led us to a table for two, never acknowledging that Joe Smith was his real name.

To make matters worse for Joe, I found the incident amusing, so during the meal, I put the fresh hibiscus behind my ear and flirted with Joe all evening. I lovingly touched his face and smoothed his black wavy hair, making Joe blush and entertaining the receptionist as she occasionally looked our way.

Mark and Luke became teenagers in Lake Wales. People commended us on how smart and good-looking they were. Of course, their accomplishments at school and at the church made their parents proud. They didn't act like spoiled PKs (preacher's kids). We had heard the stories about some ministers' children being spoiled from getting too much attention. Thank goodness, most ministers' children grow up to be decent, outstanding adults.

Our sons were expected to treat people with genuine respect. They were not to think they were more important or less important than anyone's sons in the community.

The parsonage was like a youth center, sometimes with planned parties and often with young people just dropping by to play games and talk and listen to music. Mark and Luke's friends felt welcome to hang out at our home. Letting our children feel free to entertain friends in their own home was a joy, and it kept us up-to-date on what was going on in their lives.

In small towns, almost everyone knows the minister's family, and the children grow up in a fishbowl. This can be good or bad. If they are well behaved, with manners, they are admired and well liked. The fishbowl must have been good for Mark and Luke because they made lots of good friends.

Just before they reached dating age, I reminded Joe it might be a good time to have a father-son talk with the boys. An in-depth talk about sexuality and the birds and the bees can sometimes be embarrassing to young boys, especially when the talk is coming from a parent. When they were little boys, asking questions like most children do, I had already told them the basics about sexuality. Of course, their young friends had tried to further enlighten them. They thought they knew it all until Daddy took them for the car ride.

First, Mark had the ride to the church office with his dad for the talk on *how to treat young ladies.* A year later, it was Luke's turn to take the ride. As father and son were going out the back door, Mark said, "Oh, Luke, I feel *sorry* for you."

Often, I asked God "Why me?" but I worked hard, taking long walks to try and keep my weak back recuperated from the surgeries every six months to correct the complications from the fall I had on water skis while at Keystone. When my spirits were at their lowest, it helped to remember the picture of footsteps on the sand of a beach. Pictures sometimes do speak louder than words, and this picture spoke louder to me than any deep theological thoughts.

The caption under the picture read, "One night a man had a dream. He dreamed he was walking along the beach with the Lord. Across the sky flashed scenes from his life. For each scene, he noticed two sets of footprints in the sand, one belonging to him, and the other to the Lord.

"When the last scene of his life flashed before him, he looked back at the footprints in the sand. He noticed that many times along the path of his life there was only one set of footprints. He also noticed that it happened at the very lowest and saddest times in his life.

"This really bothered him and he questioned the Lord about it. 'Lord, you said that once I decided to follow you, you'd walk with me all the way. But I have noticed that during the most troublesome times in my life, there is only one set of footprints. I don't understand why when I needed you most you would leave me.'

"The Lord replied, 'My precious, precious child, I love you and I would never leave you. During your times of trial and suffering, when you see only one set of footprints, it was then that I carried you.'"

This picture and the meaningful words made me realize that my Christian family and my Christian friends were carrying me and giving me the strength to fight for my life.

When first getting to Lake Wales, I had signed up for teaching courses at the local private college. I still wanted to finish my bachelor's degree so I could teach. My back pain became so severe and chronic that I had to drop the courses and put my educational goals on the back burner. *Will I ever be able to reach my goal?* I wondered. At the time, it was all I could do as I fought to regain my health.

It was the Christmas season, my favorite time of year, and I was home recuperating from my fourth back surgery. That night, my sons were in the Christmas program at the church, Luke being the little drummer boy and Mark singing and their dad reading the Christmas story. The music and the Christmas decorations were always beautiful at the Lake Wales church. I was home alone, feeling left out of my purpose in life. "Could things be worse for anyone?" I was thinking as I lay in bed feeling very sorry for myself. Shouldn't I be thankful for a warm, comfortable bed, friends cooking meals for me, and my wonderful family and nice parsonage home? Then, the doorbell rang. Who could it be? Everyone I knew was supposed to be at the Christmas church service.

I put on my robe and slowly moved my sore, aching body to answer the door. There, standing at my door, was a shy, humble-acting young father. His packed car was parked on the street, and the street light let me see he had a wife and a baby in the car.

The young man asked, "Is the minister home?"

"No, he has a Christmas service at the church. Do you have a problem?" I asked, sensing that he must have an urgent need.

He then told me that the gas station attendant said Reverend Smith might be able to help. "I was trying to sell our little TV at the gas station so I could have enough money to rent a room for the night. It's getting cold, and we think it best to rent a room instead of sleeping in the car with our baby."

Somehow, God gave me the gift to read people. I could judge when a needy story was made-up and when it was real. This young coal miner had left Kentucky, traveling to a job offer in Orlando. He was trying to seek a better life for himself and his family. When he got to Orlando, the job was no longer available, and his only friends there had moved. Now he was seeking an orange-picking job in the

Lake Wales groves. With only their few earthly belongings in the car, they were running out of money.

"Could we wait in the car until Reverend Smith gets home?"

"Go to the car and tell your wife to bring the baby inside out of the cold to wait."

He returned to the door saying his wife didn't want to bring the baby inside because the baby was soiled and smelly.

I sent him back to the car to insist that she could feel welcome to bring a soiled baby in my house. "I'll fix warm water in the tub so she can bathe the baby. Tell her I've had babies, and I understand when they need a bath."

With this invitation, the shy young mother came inside with her baby. Not only did the baby need a bath, it needed a fresh bottle of warm milk. While the mother bathed her baby, I washed the soured milk stains off their baby bottle and filled it with warm milk. Soon, they were comfortable, waiting in the family room for Joe to come home from the church. Of course, Joe had a surprise when he came home, and so did Mark and Luke when they found a sleeping baby in their family room.

There was room at the local inn (motel), and Joe was able to rent a warm, comfortable room for the family.

It later made me think of the Bible verse: "When you have done it for the least of these, you have done it for me" (Matt. 25:40).

While my family was at the church doing the Christmas story, God sent me the opportunity to experience the real meaning of the Christ child story. How could I continue to feel sorry for myself when I still had the opportunity to make a difference in the lives of other people?

Charley, the local wino who stayed down on his luck, came by the church almost every week, wanting a handout. Often he was given a ticket for a meal at the local McDonald's restaurant. Sometimes he just wanted to chat with Joe.

One day, Charley made a phone call to the parsonage asking for Joe. "This is . . . is . . . Charley. I . . . I . . . I need some help. Is . . . is . . . is Preacher Joe home?"

I had recently answered a phone call from one of Joe's minister friends who jokingly pretended he was a street person. And he was amused when I didn't recognize his voice. Now I thought he was trying the joke again.

"No, David, he's not home."

"My name's not . . . not . . . not David!"

By now I was laughing. "Oh, David, don't try to pull your joke on me again. I know it's you. How is Judy?"

"Ma'am, are you laugh . . . laugh . . . laughing at me? I'm not David!"

Poor Charley became so angry and frustrated that he just hung up the phone.

This was one time when my judgment of a needy person was not as keen, but Charley was really like the person who cries "Wolf, wolf" so often that no one believes him when the real thing happens.

Charley had made his call from the local fire station. Sometimes, he slipped in and picked up their phone when they were not looking. After his call to the Methodist parsonage, he told the fireman, "That Preacher Joe's wife ain't a bit of help!"

The fireman laughed about Charley's frustration with "that preacher's wife." Later, Joe explained to them how his wife thought Charley's call was a joke. They thought that was even more amusing.

Joe and the fireman tried to help Charley. They sent him off for treatments, but he always returned to his old habits.

A retired Baptist missionary called the parsonage. She hoped the church could help her adopted daughter. It was a long story about how she and her deceased husband had adopted the daughter. The baby had been left on their doorstep in India. Their daughter grew up and married a fellow countryman. The husband abused her and her children. Now she was separated from this cruel man.

When the missionary's daughter heard that her mother was sick and maybe dying, she left her children with friends in India. The friends promised to keep the children hidden from the cruel father and would take care of them until their mother returned from America. After arriving in Lake Wales, the missionary's daughter decided to enroll at the local college, and her friends in India were still willing to care for her children.

Now, Sara needed more money to finish college. The sick mother did not have the extra money needed for her daughter's college expenses.

After learning how badly Sara wanted to finish college, the church people and others in the community responded with extra help for her.

This is the rest of the story. The missionary mother died. Then Sara's friend in India informed her that the abusive man had found the hidden children. After hearing this, her American friends bought Sara plane tickets to fly back to India to rescue her children. Somehow, she stole her children from the abusive husband and made her way with them back to Lake Wales.

Sara had one semester left to finish college, and she desperately wanted to finish so she could support herself and her children.

It was during the winter season, after Christmas, and I answered the doorbell. There stood the little mother and her four children. She was crying and asking for help. I took them in, fed the hungry children, and put them to bed with a tired little mother.

Joe came home from his board meeting and found that his soft-hearted wife had taken in a mother and four children.

"What in the world are we going to do with four children? I know the mother has a room at the college, but we can't keep the children," Joe reasoned.

I agreed with Joe that we couldn't keep the children. "I just couldn't leave them out in the street tonight. Maybe the Methodist Children's Home will keep the children until the mother finishes college."

"I sure hope so. First thing in the morning, I'm on my way to the Florida Children's Home," Joe said.

The Methodist Children's Home *did* take the children! When Sara finished college, she got a job and made a home for herself and her children.

A Sunday school class gave Joe a new toy for Christmas, a monkey called Curious George. "They think I can use him for my children's stories."

From that Sunday until Joe retired, it was Joe and George telling the children's stories together. Joe and George were a famous hit with children and adults alike. Joe made up his own stories for George. Of course, George was always getting in trouble at the church.

The first Sunday with George, Joe came down from the pulpit as usual to sit with the children. "Well, children, George and I want to know what did your dad give your mother for Christmas."

One little girl said, "He gave my mommy a new toaster!"

"A new toaster! Wasn't that nice, George?" George shook his head side to side, as if to say "Noooo," and the congregation roared.

A little boy anxious for his turn yelled, "My daddy gave my mama a pretty red gown!" George shook his head up and down like "Yes, yes, yes!" The congregation roared even louder with laughter.

After a few more gift-sharing tales, Joe said, "Children, let's bow our heads for a little prayer. 'Thank you, God, for daddies and mothers and for all the gifts we share with each other. And we thank you that George has come to share stories with us too. Amen.'"

Sunday after Sunday, Joe and George shared stories with the children. All around the Florida Methodist Conference, other ministers heard about Joe and George telling church children stories. Joe and George were asked to tell a story at the Children's Home in Deland.

Even the bishop in Lakeland heard about Joe and George. When he was speaking in one of Joe's churches, the bishop joked, "I ordain George, the monkey, and now he will get half of Joe's salary."

One Sunday, after shaking hands with everyone leaving the morning church service, Joe noticed that Mr. Carter was still standing alone at the back of the sanctuary. He was a quiet fellow, very wealthy but without airs, never flaunting his blessings. The Carters owned a large air-conditioning business in Washington DC. His business supplied many of the government buildings in Washington.

Joe knew it must be something important that Mr. Carter wanted to speak to his minister about. And it was!

"Joe, would you consider taking our house for your parsonage?" he asked.

"Sure, but why do you want to give us your house? You've already given the parsonage we live in, and it's nice."

"We don't use the pool, and your family will use the pool. Swimming will be good for Gloria's back therapy. My wife wants to live further out of town. We're building a house with the same floor plan but without a pool. Instead of a pool, I'm going to have a barn built big enough to store all of her stuff." Mrs. Carter was extra thrifty. She saved everything!

After a few months, we moved into the special house. The lovely home sat on four lots, surrounded by a high, private hedge. There were entrance gates and a wide circular drive. It was quite an impressive parsonage, probably more impressive than any other parsonage in the state at that time. The front entrance had double french doors. Inside were chandeliers, huge mirrors, walk-in closets, and spacious rooms. From the living room were sliding glass doors that opened to an indoor patio and that in turn opened to a large pool area. Beyond the screened-in pool, which was surrounded by an outdoor patio and gardens, was a large game room.

It was a house that needed to be shared with family and friends. Our first open house was a Christmas party for the church membership. Hundreds of people attended. Everyone wanted to see the newly decorated parsonage. A local furniture store had helped update the parsonage furniture. With the Christmas decorations and new furniture, it was beautiful!

While living in this special parsonage, we hosted a lot of parties and dinners and had visits from relatives and out-of-town friends. With Mark and Luke's friends, the house was filled with the excitement of teenagers. The pool and game room became the youth group's special place to hang out.

Joe worried that the extra activity would be hard on me while I was recuperating from back surgeries. I told him, "No, it's a joy! I love knowing where my sons are most of the time and who they're with. We are so blessed having this special parsonage as our home. It's wonderful seeing young people having so much fun! They love the pool and the game room. When I get tired, I just go inside and leave the chaperoning to the youth director."

Now I had a home that was fit for a queen, but I would have given it up in a moment for better health. There were so many things I wanted to do but couldn't. I had to learn to make myself useful in spite of the painful health problem. I taught myself to crochet baby blankets for all the new babies being born into the growing families of my sisters and brothers. Handmade blankets also made special gifts for our friends' new babies. I did the crocheting while sitting in a large reclining chair and sometimes while in bed.

The younger women in the church wanted to start a circle and take on a good project. This was something I could do. I helped them start the circle, and I told them about a nearby migrant camp that might need some help. To find out what the camp might need, I asked one of the young ladies to drive with me to it. At the camp, we found that another church group had built a nursery building so the babies and young children could have a comfortable place to stay while the mothers, along with the fathers, worked in the fields picking vegetables or fruits. We found out they could use clothing or any kind of household items. The items were given out from the nursery's storage room. Also, volunteers took care of the children.

One day, when we went back to the migrant camp nursery to take items that the circle of women had collected, I noticed a crying baby in a crib. I picked up the baby and began comforting him in a rocking chair. The baby was pulling at his ear.

I told the nursery helper, "This baby has an ear infection. Be sure to tell the mother to take him to the clinic for medicine when she returns."

I couldn't leave the sick baby crying, so I laid his painful ear against my warm chest and rocked him to sleep. Then I gently laid him in a crib with a silent prayer before I left that nursery.

The women of the young circle continued helping the migrant camp for years, and that warmed my heart. Those Spanish immigrants were probably not much different from some of our former ancestors who had migrated from other countries to find a better life in America. They too must have looked forward to finding a way that their children could receive a better education and improve their standard of living.

I always told my sisters and brothers, "The way out of ignorance and poverty is to get a good education. If you can't go to college, then educate yourself. Read, read, and read! Libraries are full of good books." This was easy for me because I loved to read.

During his senior year of high school, Mark entered the community college on the early entrance program. He could still live at home, be with his high school friends, and have the honor of graduating with his senior class. By the time Mark marched in his high school graduation, he had finished two years of college. That was quite an accomplishment for a seventeen-year-old.

The next fall, his dad and I stood by our driveway, waving goodbye as Mark drove away to Florida State University in Tallahassee. He never saw the tears flowing down his mother's face as he drove away.

I said, "This is worse than the day he went across the street for first grade. Now, home will never be the same without both of my sons."

"We have to let them grow up, Gloria. Just think, there will be fewer clothes to wash." Joe tried to sound brave as his voice cracked with some emotion too.

With arms around each other, we walked back inside the house. We had a glass of tea and talked about our son's growing up years. At least we would have Luke with us for another year before experiencing a completely empty nest.

Children are like little birds. They grow wings of their own and leave their parents' nest in search of freedom and their own grains of fortune. Some are cautious and keep flying high while others sometimes linger too long on the ground and are caught by a predator. Would Mark remember what he had been taught at home, to know right from wrong and how to keep safe?

On a Sunday morning in April of 1981, Joe informed the congregation that his wife had a devotional in *The Upper Room*. He said. "I want you to know that my wife, Gloria, has written a devotional for *The Upper Room*, and you can read it this coming Tuesday, April 28. As some of you may know, *The Upper Room* goes around the world in over forty languages. It touches the hearts of millions of people. No matter how many sermons I preach, I'll probably never touch as many lives as my wife has done with this one special devotion. Her words express how she has reached out to God for strength when faced with serious health problems."

It was special having my husband say such kind words because I had felt that my personal accomplishments had been interrupted with pain and despair. With the back problem and all the complications, I had suffered four back surgeries while in Lake Wales. It took all my strength to support my husband in his work and my sons in their school work. Life had to go on!

Since I walked a lot to strengthen my weak back muscles, Joe often walked with me after lunch or in the late evenings. One evening after dark, we were walking around the beautiful Lake Wales. We could reach the Lake's cemented walking path easily since it was just a block from our house. The path stretched a few miles all around the lake. This particular night was one of those perfect Florida spring evenings with a soft, cool breeze. Suddenly, we both stopped and looked at each other.

"Do you see that moving light across the lake?" I asked Joe.

"Yeah, but I can't figure out what it is."

We stood for several minutes watching it slowly move just a few feet over the lake. It was a perfectly round moonlike light, except it was three times the size of a full moon. It didn't make a sound, just slowly moved back and forth several times, like it was searching for something at the edge of the backyards on the lake. Then, all of a sudden, it blinked out; it disappeared without us seeing it go up or down! No, we didn't see any windows in it, and we didn't see any little creatures from Mars. But we did see something that was definitely an unexplainable light for us.

After seeing that sight, I never questioned all the stories about people seeing unidentifiable objects. I know some sightings may still be exaggerated tales for attention. Joe and I didn't need that type of attention, so we didn't go around telling other people about our particular experience of seeing that big moving ball of light.

Each spring at the beginning of National Family Week, Joe had a service to celebrate families. During the Sunday morning church service, there was a time for couples to renew wedding vows. First, all the couples married for fifty years or more were asked to come up front and stand before the altar. It was always impressive to see how many couples in the church had celebrated their fifty years of marriage. Next, all the couples married for twenty-five years or more were asked to stand.

Then all the younger couples stood. I stood with Joe. After all the years of marriage were recognized, the wedding vows were renewed.

Many people expressed that this service, renewing wedding vows, strengthened their marriages. Joe had this service in all of his churches over the years. It was a way to help families stay united and happy.

It is beautiful to see couples happy on their wedding day. Joe and I experienced many beautiful, happy weddings. Some were big, elaborate celebrations, some small and sweet, but all precious. But the most beautiful celebrations were couples celebrating their fiftieth wedding anniversary, surrounded by grateful grown children and lots of good friends.

Our family stood together in the parsonage backyard with sad faces and tears as we buried Sam, our little black five-pound Chihuahua. We buried him under the beautiful azalea bush. It had been a dozen years that little Sam had been a best friend to each of us. As the mascot of three parsonages, he had faithfully welcomed and touched the hearts of people. He had spent his life watching Mark and Luke grow up into handsome, lovable young men. He had touched their deepest sensitivities and taught them to love all creatures, great or small.

Mark had been Sam's favorite. It was good that he was home for spring break to help bury Sam. It is never easy for a family or anyone else when a loved pet dies. This experience taught us to be understanding and sensitive to people when they grieved the loss of a pet.

Luke followed his brother's footsteps by entering the community college on the Early Entry Program during his senior year of high school. That fall, we were not surprised when he chose Florida State University. Brothers were back together. Like most brothers, they got on each other's nerves sometimes, but not so much that they didn't want the company and support of each other.

Luke had a witty, outgoing personality, and people were always asking, "Will Luke go into the ministry?" Besides being charming, Luke was tall, dark, and handsome. We never pressured our sons about their choice of a career. They were free to choose their own careers.

Life never stays the same very long. After eight wonderful years in Lake Wales, the bishop called. It seemed the longer living in a place, the harder it was telling dear friends goodbye. It was eight years of sharing all the special moments in people's lives: the joys, the sorrows, the weddings, the births, the break-ups, and the deaths.

The church members gave a wonderful going-away party and a generous gift. They heard we were moving to a parsonage by a large lake, so they gave us a pontoon boat!

The McClendons, a retired couple in the Lake Wales church, had impressed us so much. We could never forget how they shared their lake beach with the young people in the church. Ministers don't have to always set a good example for others; sometimes, others can set a good example for a minister and his family.

Joe and I often said, "When we retire, we want to be just like the McClendons, sharing our time and our home with the church young people."

Besides the McClendons, we would miss the Whites, the Crews, the Bryans, the Curtises, the Geils, the Hardmans, the Hicks, the Howells, the Lassitters, the McGills, the Whitmires, the Coopers, the Sebrings, and many others who would remain in our hearts.

Mark and Luke felt like they were taking Lake Wales with them to Tallahassee. Many of their Lake Wales friends were going to Florida State University too. Even their girlfriends were going to Florida State. The church's youth group seniors were a close-knit group. How long would their friendships last?

LEESBURG, FLORIDA: 1981-1986

AFTER ARRIVING IN Leesburg, we were given another party, a welcome reception at the Morrison church. Our sons stood with us, meeting and shaking the hands with the new congregation. There were hundreds of new names and faces to learn.

Morrison United Methodist Church had a long history, starting back in 1857 with the Methodist Circuit Riders.

The first missionary sent from Florida in 1887 was from this church. Nannie B. Gaines was called from Morrison to be the first principal of the Hiroshima Girls School in Hiroshima, Japan. She served there for forty years!

The present sanctuary building was built in 1924, and it was sort of like "This old house once knew my children." It was not only old but was bursting at the seams with new growth. There were three Sunday morning services with many retirees from up North.

Joe preached all three services. Sometimes, Don Hanna, the young associate minister, preached one of the services. There were children at the first service and the last service, so George the Monkey helped with the children's story.

Being a little late to get a good seat, I had to sit on a folding chair in the back of the church. With that view of the whole sanctuary, I saw this petite, older lady literally stand up in the back pew so she could see Joe and George as he told the children's story.

At home while having lunch, I told Joe, "George is as interesting to some adults as he is to the children. You will not believe what I saw happen in church this morning. An older lady couldn't see from the back pew, so she stood up in the pew."

One day, Joe came home excited over buying a buggy. "We'll need to take a summer trip to upstate New York to get it. Mr. Brown still has it up there on his farm."

Joe and I decided to extend our trip to Canada with our sons. On the way, we stopped in Washington to view the Capitol building and the White House. It made us think of Mr. Wheeler, the Kite father who took his children there in a camper school bus. We stopped for a night to see the Amish farms in Pennsylvania as well as many other sites along the way. We also spent a couple of nights with our Lake Wales friends, the Geils, at their Silver Bay cottage at Lake George, New York.

On the way home, we got a lot of attention on the road, pulling a trailer with an antique buggy on it!

The buggy finally made it to the family farm in Georgia. Joe and I took a buggy ride down the red clay roads near the family farm. The farm horse did a good job pulling the buggy and getting us safely back to the barn.

Joe knew the church was having growing pains. He told me one evening, "Things are just getting too crowded in the old sanctuary. Some of the longtime members are mentioning that we need a building program. Maybe it's time to put things in motion at the next board meeting and appoint a committee."

The new building committee was formed! And it was all men. Some of the committee's wives and I were talking. We didn't know if the men would think of everything that women would like in a new sanctuary, so we decided to have a luncheon meeting.

All the wives of the building committee were present at the luncheon, and there was a lot of discussion about plans for the new sanctuary. It was discussed and decided that the new sanctuary should have a high steeple, a bell tower, and a beautiful bride's room. Several other special ideas were mentioned. The plans were made!

Someone said, "Ladies, tonight we go home and do a lot of *pillow talk*!"

For a long time, Joe and the men on the building committee never knew how the first seeds for the new sanctuary were planted.

Ground was broken on March 18, 1984. Members were asked to make suggestions as to what should be included and to present pictures of churches they admired. When the plans for the building were completed, they were posted for all to see. The plans included a high steeple with a colonial style building! By now all the wishes of the women as well as the men's ideas were included.

Progress on the church was watched closely by members, and many pictures were taken. Joe invited the congregation to view the progress on Sunday afternoons.

On Sunday mornings during announcement times, Joe would say, "No construction is being done today, so come on out this afternoon at five o'clock, and I will show you the work completed this past week."

Joe was enjoying every moment of his building project. In his youth, when he was fighting the call to be a minister instead of a contractor, Joe never dreamed that he would have the opportunity to build churches.

While Joe was busy with the building program and all the other pastoral duties, I was hired part-time by the church as the director of volunteers. I spent many hours organizing the program and coordinating the volunteers. Of course, the part-time position grew into a full-time job before long, but the salary always continues to be part-time pay in churches with a building program. I didn't complain because I enjoyed the work. I still needed time to manage my chronic back pain by taking long walks and long afternoon rest so that I could attend a dinner party or some other evening activity.

I organized the Blue Coats, a group of volunteers to help the ministers with visiting shut-ins, nursing homes, and hospitals. It was fun to organize parties and receptions for groups in the church. I also taught foreign people in the community to read and speak English. I organized help for needy children.

Given my interest in a little five-year-old foster child with a family in our church, Joe got worried when I mentioned adoption. Little Jessica had dark brown hair and big brown eyes, and she often begged to come home with me. She couldn't always get special attention since there were several other children at the foster home. I found myself bringing her home for some of the special attention that she seemed to need. She loved for me to read her a children's story, and after lunch, she would usually fall peacefully asleep after two or three stories.

With both sons away in college, I was too busy to let the empty-nest syndrome affect me much. Besides, I was mothering children all over the community. I finally convinced Joe that we needed to go to a Social Services meeting about children who needed to be adopted.

When Mark heard about his mother interested in adopting a child, he said on the phone, "Dad, get Mom a dog! She's missing Sam."

I picked up another phone and heard Mark's remark.

"No, I'm not getting another dog right now. I can't get a dog with alligators sunning in our backyard by the lake. The other day, I watched as one tried to pull the neighbor's dog into the lake. Now Shooter has a broken leg. But I do miss you and Luke! I just keep busy."

One Saturday, we went to the Social Services meeting about children who needed parents. We didn't know that the social workers were going to include children to speak at the meeting and tell the visiting adults why they needed or wanted parents. These were children around eight, nine or, ten years old.

A little nine-year-old boy stole everyone's heart when he spoke so maturely and convincingly about why he wanted to be adopted. He told how he had an alcoholic father and a mother who didn't want him in her life, describing it without shame or shyness. It was like "I'm special, and I want to be loved, and someone needs my love."

He said, "I want a nice daddy and mama, and I don't want a daddy that drinks alcohol."

We came to find out about Jessica, and we found out that a psychologist and his wife had already started a process to adopt Jessica. We could only be happy that Jessica would have a good home.

All week we discussed the little boy who spoke so eloquently about his wanting a family. "Wouldn't he grow up making a great speaker for whatever cause he wanted to lift up? Maybe he'll be a minister," I commented.

Joe said, "Maybe we should think about adopting him now that Jessica isn't available."

"I'm not sure. I have two sons, and I've just always wanted a little girl. But I'll pray about it. I really think he's a special little boy, and I want him to have good parents who will love him."

The next Sunday, Joe had an illustration in his sermon about the little boy and how he brought tears to the eyes of his listeners as he pleaded his case of needing a good home. Joe said, "Thanksgiving is near, and we can all be thankful for good homes where children can grow up with security and love."

After that Sunday morning service, a couple about our age stood waiting for Joe to finish greeting the people as they exited the sanctuary. They wanted to know how they could reach the social worker because they were interested in the little boy he mentioned in his sermon. It worked out that the nice couple adopted the little boy. It seems God does work in mysterious ways sometimes! It wasn't meant for us to adopt those children, but we experienced the joy of knowing they were safer and happier in good homes.

Across the street, behind the church property, was a neighborhood. In a rented house lived a Vietnamese family. I noticed the children as they played on the sidewalk. It was cold, and they had no shoes on their little feet. I decided they needed some attention and help, so I crossed the street to check on them.

The family of a father, a mother, and six little boys had just moved to Leesburg from a camp in Cambodia. They had been in that camp after the war ended in Vietnam. A smaller Methodist church in town had financed their plane tickets to America and found the father a job at a mushroom farm. Church mission finished.

But the family had a lot of needs. Neither of the parents could speak English. I offered to teach them. With the help of church friends, I got beds for them as well as other badly needed items. They were sleeping on the floor and living out of boxes.

After observing the mother was cooking on a little grill on the back porch, I put a request in the church newsletter: "Family needs a stove." The next day, a nice used stove was donated.

At first, the children called me Mother Minister. Later, they called me Mommy Smith. Joe was Daddy Smith. Those names stuck, and the children grew up calling us Daddy and Mommy Smith.

One morning, Nguyen, the children's mother, came to my office at the church for her English lesson, and she was crying.

"Oh, Nguyen, what's wrong? Is one of the children sick?" I asked.

"No, no," she said, patting her stomach while trying to express herself in English. "A baby!"

"You're going to have another baby?"

She nodded yes. Having six little rambunctious boys was a big job for any mother, and now this poor little mother was expecting another baby. I needed to say something to help this distraught mother.

"Nguyen, maybe God is going to give you a little girl!"

"No, no, no, boys, boys, boys," She said it like all she could have were boys.

I thought of something else that might cheer my upset friend. "Nguyen, we will have a party for you. It's called a baby shower. My friends will come and bring lots of gifts for your baby."

Now Nguyen smiled.

A few months later, Kim was born. A proud, smiling mother put the baby girl in my arms and said, "Kim, your other mother."

"Nguyen, she's beautiful!"

When the parents decided to have Kim baptized, they asked me to be her godmother. She wore the baptism gown that had been handmade by our boys' Great-grandmother Smith. No other child outside of our family had worn that beautiful white gown. She would always be a part of the Smith family as well as her own Lam family. I would love this child forever. My family would not have to worry about me adopting a foster child. I had Kim and her six brothers to mentor and love.

The Lam children observed how our sons went to college. They grew up wanting to go to college too. *And they did!* All seven finished college, and four earned graduate degrees. Hai and Nguyen Lam as well as the Smiths were proud of their children. The Lam children always showed their appreciation and friendship to us and to our family. They also learned to take care of one another as well as their parents. They were truly an American success story.

Mark graduated from law school in December 1984. Of course, Joe and I were proud parents, but Joe's father was the proudest. He admitted that he had hoped his son would grow up to be a lawyer. Maybe that explained the tears rolling down his face as he watched Mark receive his degree. Those were tears of joy! Sometimes people watch their own dreams materialize with a child or a grandchild.

Mark was engaged to Martha Geils during his last year of law school. A few weeks after his graduation, they had their wedding at the Lake Wales church. Martha's parents had moved their family from New Jersey to Lake Wales, and they had joined the Lake Wales church while we were there. Joe had been their pastor. Of course, Mark and Martha had lots of friends in Lake Wales, so that is where they wanted to have their wedding. They had spent their youth and high school years there. Both were now graduates of Florida State University.

Who would Martha pick for her flower girl? My sisters and brothers had young children, and all six of the little girls wanted to be in Mark and Martha's wedding.

Martha didn't want to disappoint any of the little girls, so I came up with a new idea. Let all the little girls be called rice girls. They can dress alike and give out the rice (birdseed) at the reception. Martha liked the idea and didn't choose a flower girl. She had "rice girls" instead.

The wedding was a few days after Christmas, so the little girls wore red taffeta dresses with white stockings and black patent leather shoes. They carried the rice in little red-ribbon-decorated baskets.

The bride was beautiful! Her bridesmaids were lovely in dark green. And the little girls (Mark's young cousins) added a special touch to the wedding pictures. Someone said, "Besides the bride, the little girls stole the show."

Of course, Daddy Joe went back to Lake Wales and performed our son's wedding.

One Sunday, Joe and George were entertaining the children and adults alike when the unthinkable happened. Joe got too close to the altar candle and caught George's tail on fire.

Someone in the front pew yelled, "George's tail is on fire!" Joe looked around to see if that was so, and with George hooked around his neck, he stood in shock as a choir member used her robe's stole to smother the blaze.

You could hear the *ooohs* from the congregation as if they were feeling George's pain. The children sat looking serious and silent as Joe said to the associate minister, "Would you please take George to the emergency room and get help for his burn?"

By this time, George's tail smelled up the sanctuary. Don, the associate minister, hurried out the back door with him. Joe closed the children's story with a prayer, and the rest of the service went on as usual.

The next Sunday, the children anxiously came down for the children's story, seeing that George was back. George's tail had been repaired with a piece of matching fur.

Joe began the story with a report, "Well, George's tail has healed nicely! Isn't it good to have George back at church after major surgery on his tail?"

I wasn't feeling well that Sunday and was listening to the service on Leesburg's local radio station. Oh my goodness, does Joe realize how that sounds to strangers listening on the radio? They don't know that he is talking about a toy monkey. I felt embarrassed that Joe kept repeating how well George had recovered from his *tail surgery*!

I couldn't wait for Joe to get home. I met him at the door. This topic couldn't wait until Monday! "Do you know how you came across on the radio during the children's story saying, 'Isn't it good to have George back at church after major surgery on his tail?'"

Joe can laugh at himself. He chuckled and said, "How funny it must be to think of someone listening on a car radio and hear a weird minister talk about his church member's tail surgery and how he's healing nicely."

Joe had a good laugh, and I joined him as I thought about the humor of the situation. Joe later told that story to family and friends, and it always got a laugh.

Spring was busy with another family wedding. Now, our son Luke was marrying his childhood sweetheart, Karen Whitmire. I had my answer in wondering how long the Lake Wales young people's group would stick together. Luke and Karen had both finished their degrees at Florida State University. Joe needed to perform another wedding in the beloved Lake Wales church. Karen's family, the Whitmires and Hardmans, were longtime members of that church. Joe had been the pastor for Karen's grandparents as well as her parents and other family members.

In spring colors, the wedding party was lovely but not more beautiful than the little rice girls in pink dresses and white stockings and shoes. They carried little Easter baskets with the wrapped birdseed. Again, the photographer went wild, placing the little girls around the bride and groom for pictures. Not even the lovely bridesmaids had been made over as much as the little girls had. Karen was a beautiful bride and Luke a handsome groom.

With a large reception in the fellowship hall, hundreds of friends and relatives enjoyed celebrating the occasion. Friends from the Morrison church as well as the Lake Wales church attended the wedding and the reception. The little Lam boys giggled in amusement as Luke pulled the garter off his bride's leg. Luke had giggled at his aunt's wedding; now little boys were giggling at his.

A few weeks later, a large crowd had gathered on Main Street in Leesburg, watching the crane lift the new church steeple. I was there with my camera. Joe was running around trying to organize everything for the big event. He had just called the contractor's company that sent the crane. The crane man wanted them to know that he thought the crane was too small to lift the tall, heavy steeple!

Joe yelled up to the crane man, "They say it's okay!"

The crane man started raising the steeple. It began to swing and wobble! Then, the crane man yelled back down to Joe, "Go call them again and tell them it's just not going to work!"

Joe called again.

He yelled up again to the crane man, "They said to go ahead with it because they have it all figured out, and it will work!"

The man said, "Tell all the people to move back. I'm going ahead with it, but it's probably going to fall!"

The steeple swung and wobbled as the crane roared, trying to lift it. Then it fell! People were running and screaming! Thank God, no one was hurt.

A few weeks later, the steeple was rebuilt, and a bigger crane was sent to lift it. This time it made it, and the impressive steeple was placed on the new church sanctuary. The board members' wives smiled.

Norma Hendricks, columnist for the *Leesburg Commercial,* said in her column dated July 29, 1985, "The Rev. Joe Smith of the Morrison United Methodist Church has kept such close watch on every brick and pane of glass going into the new sanctuary on Leesburg's Main Street that it is a wonder he didn't get accidentally plastered into a wall. The target date for the congregation to move into the new sanctuary is now September 8, but the minister reported Sunday that the pigeons have already moved into the facade of the church . . . Perhaps the Methodist minister could do some proselytizing in reverse, and persuade the Methodist pigeons to become Baptists."

All the plans, all the building committee meetings, all the financial campaigns to meet the rising cost of building, all the dealing with contractors and carpenters, and all the building problems and conflicts had been solved. Now, Joe rejoiced with his building committee and congregation that the job was finished.

On Main Street in downtown Leesburg, Florida, stood the largest and most beautiful church in the Florida United Methodist Conference. Each Sunday was a day of pride and excitement as the crowds filled the new sanctuary. Joe no longer had to have three services to accommodate the crowds. He was back to only two services, with Sunday school in between. The church was also used for community events, district events, and conference events as well as beautiful weddings, baptisms, and stately funerals.

One group of older ladies in the church wanted to make chrismons for the church Christmas tree. I had a book of patterns for chrismons, and those talented ladies used my copied patterns to make the most beautiful handmade decorations I had ever seen in any church. Joe had to go to Orlando to find a tree large enough to hold all the handmade chrismons. With the help of John Gill III, the associate, and Tom DeWitt, the organist, they found the perfect tree. That first Christmas in the new sanctuary was extra beautiful with that special tree.

Another circle of young women was formed in the Leesburg church like the one I had helped form in Lake Wales. They also asked my help to find a good project for their new circle. I suggested they help Family Services with collecting new stuffed animals for children. When young, insecure children come into the system, they usually need a soft teddy bear or doggy to cuddle and sleep with. The social workers were very delighted over the circle's project. Later, after moving away from Leesburg, I heard that the women were still collecting stuffed animals for foster children. This is the kind of planted seed that makes the work worthwhile. Many ministers and their mates start projects that continue long after they move on to other situations. Sometimes, they never see the results of some of their work, but when they do, it feels good.

While in Leesburg, I had not only worked part-time at the church, but I had started a little home project for children. In my little home office, I wrote monthly letters to a list of children. These were letters (short stories, actually) from Annie Elf! The little elf became very popular, and the list of children getting the letters grew until there were children receiving the letters in almost all of the states and some foreign countries. Local kindergarten teachers asked me to visit and read an Annie Elf letter to the children. A reporter wrote an article about the letters in the local newspaper. Parents and grandparents sent stamp money for the letters, and I kept writing the little letter stories. I received back letters and drawings from children and words of appreciation from parents. These were not religious letters, just fun stories with a touch of love for all children.

One child on my list was a little ten-year-old girl in Orlando who had had a heart transplant. Like a lot of children who early in life have to deal with a serious illness, she was wise beyond her years. She wrote her little soul out to Annie Elf. And there was an Orlando newspaper reporter who wrote articles that kept the community informed about this precious child's condition. When Jeanie had a second heart transplant after the first one was rejected, the reporter let her describe the process in her own words. Jeanie had expressed to the reporter that she wanted to grow up to be a writer just like her.

Before Jeanie went back in the hospital, Annie Elf sent her a new pair of bedroom shoes and a child's umbrella. I had paid a local artist to paint a flower as well as Jeanie's name on the umbrella.

From the hospital, Jeanie wrote Annie Elf a sad letter.

She wrote, "Dear Annie Elf, I liked my new bedroom shoes very much and my umbrella was my favorite thing, but someone stole my shoes and my umbrella while we were out of the room for my physical therapy treatments. I know you are not a real elf and I want to know if you have children, but I always want you to send me the elf letters even if I know you are a real person."

Of course, I continued sending Jeanie the elf letters, and I replaced her umbrella and bedroom shoes that had been stolen. Since her shoes and umbrella were in a bag on the floor, maybe a cleaning lady just thought they were trash and threw them away. It was hard to wrap my mind about the kind of person who would steal from a child heart patient. I knew from the reporter's articles that the child's parents were having a hard time financially, and they couldn't afford extras for their sick child. They had already lost their home trying to meet all the medical expenses for their child.

A few months after Jeanie returned to Orlando from her second heart surgery, her reporter friend wrote the sad article that included Jeanie's picture: "Jeanie has lost her fight for life."

Jeanie and I had never met, but our souls had met, and the news of her death touched me deeply.

Jeanie's mother wrote me a thank-you note, and I wrote an elf story letter about a beautiful butterfly in Jeanie's memory.

When certain big news events happen, like the assassination of an important person, most people remember where they were and what they were doing at that moment they heard about it. It was January 28, 1986, and I had decided to stay home to watch the Space Shuttle coverage on television. Through the years, I had kept up with all the important events with the space program. While watching and listening to the countdown for the space shuttle *Challenger* to launch, I walked out to my front yard. Several times, I had a good view from my yard of past launches. As I looked in the direction of the Kennedy Space Center, I knew something was not right. I was witnessing a strange smoke plume, so I quickly walked back inside the house to the television. At that moment, the television was silent as the announcer at the space center seemed to be going through a period of shock himself. Soon, news of the accident was shared with the nation. A massive explosion had taken place, and all seven crew members were killed. Many Americans had been watching this launch with all the media coverage about the first teacher in space, Christa McAuliffe, who was on board for the space project experience. After that space project accident, I could never again watch a launch without feeling tense and prayerful for the crew in the space shuttle.

Joe was writing a sermon in his lovely new office in the back of the new sanctuary when he got a call from his district superintendent. "Joe, the bishop is requesting that you and Gloria come for a meeting with him in Lakeland."

Joe's first thought was *Maybe he wants to congratulate me for getting the new sanctuary built. Surely he isn't thinking about moving us. We've just been in the new sanctuary a few months.*

"Why does the bishop want to meet with us?" Joe asked the district superintendent with concern in his voice. "Surely, he's not planning to move us, is he?"

"I'm sorry, Joe, but I think that is what he wants to talk with you about. The bishop's cabinet has been meeting. I told them that the Leesburg church is not ready for you to move. And I told them you've not had time to enjoy the fruits of your labor after just moving into the new sanctuary. I also informed him that a move wouldn't be easy for Gloria."

Joe was silent. This news had caught him off guard. The superintendent continued talking, "He still wants to talk with you, Joe. Bishop has a large South Florida church with some problems that could split the congregation if the right minister isn't sent there. It seems he's picked you for that job."

Joe was in no mood to have the honor of going to the largest church in the Florida conference to solve their problems.

On Monday morning, we went to the bishop's office with a balky attitude. My attitude was worse than Joe's because I knew that Joe was not ready to move from his new sanctuary and a congregation that appreciated him and his family.

"This bishop is getting old and maybe a little senile, thinking we need to move," I said angrily to Joe on the way to Lakeland.

The bishop was of the old school, thinking that a minister should move after being at a church for four or five years. Joe felt like churches grew more with longer appointments. Besides, if a congregation was happy and the minister was happy, it provided a mobile society with some stability to have a pastor with a long ministry.

The bishop and two district superintendents met with us in Lakeland at the bishop's office. As the bishop explained his position about why he needed Joe at another church, neither Joe nor I seemed pleased. I could see the disappointed look on Joe's face. Joe was not emotionally ready to leave the Morrison church and his present congregation.

I lost my cool when the bishop and the superintendent of the Melbourne district tried to impress me with a pictorial directory, pointing out the lovely steeple on the Stuart First United Methodist Church. We already had the steeple of our dreams. How dare they try to impress me with that steeple picture? I literally threw the book across the table at them!

For a few seconds, you could have heard a pin drop in that room. Even the bishop sat speechless. I was even amazed at myself. Joe never mentioned my actions because he knew I had expressed what he had felt like doing. He was just surprised that his quiet, reserved, mannerly wife showed the bishop her true feelings and inner strength.

The happiness and rights of my family always came first, before the church or any bishop.

As the Morrison congregation heard the news about Joe's moving, the people expressed their disappointment. One of the leaders in the church even called the bishop to complain, letting the bishop know that the congregation wanted Joe to stay longer at Morrison. But it didn't change the stubborn bishop's new appointment for Joe.

The church hostess and her committee had planned a beautiful farewell party for us. It was good they had an abundance of party food because they had some unexpected guest, the radio congregation!

Many of the people who had listened to Joe's sermons on the radio stood in the long reception line that reached down the sidewalk into the fellowship hall. They patiently waited their turn for a chance to express their appreciation for the man who had become their pastor.

The radio program that ran on Sunday mornings just before the church service was a black gospel music hour. With their radios already on, people continued listening to Joe's sermons. The radio guests were well-dressed men in their nice suits and ladies wearing hats.

Joe was surprised and humbled that these dear people came to say goodbye and wish him well, along with hundreds from the church congregation. Until now, he had never realized that his radio sermons had reached so many people. Besides, he had never tried to be an evangelist. Maybe that was the reason these people were impressed with his sermons! His sermons spoke to the everyday joys and problems of life. People always seemed to know he wasn't just an average Joe.

Joe often said, "When encouraged by some great people, it helps me be a better person and a better pastor."

Joe was encouraged by members like the Aults, the Whites, the Wagners, the Taylors, the Pearsons, the Montgomerys, the Listons, the Lenharts, the Knowles, the Jansens, the Huxes, the Hogans, the Huffers, the Herlongs, the Greggs, the Goldsteins, the Burnseds, and the Dewitts. Many of these people kept in touch with us and continued our friendships.

STUART, FLORIDA: 1986-1991

THE FIRST UNITED Methodist Church of Stuart was in a fast-growing part of South Florida. Stuart had once been a quiet little fishing village, surrounded by rivers and the nearby ocean. Now, it had become a fast-paced community. Down the road was the famous Palm Beach, with all the tourist activity. Stuart had its share of extra winter visitors.

Before moving, Joe and I drove down to Stuart from Leesburg, needing a peek at the church and parsonage. It was a Saturday afternoon in June, and things were quieter in the summer with most of the winter visitors back up North. The winter crowds would remind one of geese, flying back up North as soon as the seasons changed. People and geese don't like weather too hot or too cold!

"This place has no trees," Joe commented as we made a turn on Ocean Boulevard.

Of course, Stuart is very tropical looking but without royal palms on the main street like we remembered seeing when we first saw Homestead. The downtown section was not too impressive. One had to go over by the river and nearer to the ocean to see Stuart's beauty.

Back on Kanner Highway, by the side of the busy road, sat the church plant with a large parking lot in front of it.

"Looks like all cement," I remarked as we drove into the parking lot. "Well, the stained glass steeple is nice, skinny and tall but not as impressive as Morrison's," I continued.

"And the church sanctuary looks like a damn whale!" Joe laughed, probably to keep from crying.

After sitting for a few minutes, silently viewing our new appointment, Joe said, "We just have to remember there will be good people here like everywhere, and they will need a pastor." Joe became positive and more philosophical.

"Sure, I know. There are always good people and new friends to meet wherever we go," I agreed.

It's not that the Stuart church plant was so bad or even old like the Keystone church was, but it just didn't measure up to the new sanctuary in Leesburg or even to our former church in Lake Wales.

From the church, we drove over to Carolina Drive to have a peek at our future home. Things went from bad to worse. "How will I live through this?" I said in a sad voice.

We were used to a lovely home in a nice neighborhood, and it was hard to accept this average-looking house. We had a new two-story parsonage by a lake in Leesburg. Nothing is cheap in South Florida, but this house had that older, added-on look. It certainly didn't measure up to what we had become used to in Lake Wales or Leesburg.

"Do you want to go back to Georgia?" Joe asked sounding like that's what he was ready to do. "Dad will always make room for me in his candy brokerage business."

"No, I don't want to do that. I'll adjust. You have forty years of ministry planned, and I know you want to finish the job. We can do what we usually do, work to make the place better and love people." I tried hard to be positive.

When there is a drastic change in an environment, even a dedicated minister and his family have to let time heal the disappointments of change. From past experiences, we knew every place had its positives as well as its negatives, just as people did. We knew it takes more than a house to make a home. And it takes more than a building to make a church. It takes good people!

Joe and I had not expected to move, so we had planned a fiftieth anniversary party for Joe's parents. The invitations already had been sent. It was the same date as the first Sunday Joe was to be in the Stuart pulpit. This was an important time in the lives of Joe's parents, so this was a time when family had to be put before church work. Joe's parents certainly needed their family, especially their only son, at their special celebration. The new associate minister could speak on that Sunday and tell the congregation that they would meet the new senior pastor on the following Sunday. Most people would understand our circumstances. And they did. The next Sunday evening, they gave us a delightful welcome. Ralph Gudeman, the talented choir director, had a wonderful voice, and we were welcomed with song.

A few months later, Joe had a sermon titled "Bloom Where You Are Planted!" Later that year, I was asked to give a devotional at the ministers' mates retreat, and Joe's sermon gave me an idea. I titled the devotional "Bloom Where You Are Appointed!" I wrote the devotional thinking that was what I needed to do, encourage myself as well as other ministers' wives to bloom and adjust in new situations. It must have touched a nerve for the other ministers' mates as I held up a rosebud and gave them the devotional. Later, the Minister's Mates Committee met and decided to have T-shirts printed with a rosebud on it and the words "Bloom Where You Are Appointed!" The shirts were sold all over the Florida United Methodist Conference.

Later, they appeared in other states around the Southeast. Most people never knew who penned the words "Bloom Where You Are Appointed!"

When Joe saw a shirt at Lake Junaluska, a United Methodist retreat center in Waynesville, North Carolina, he smiled to himself, knowing that his wife had finally adjusted to Stuart. He knew I loved the people, the shops, and the beach.

Joe flattered me by saying, "Going to the beach often has made you look like the suntanned girl you were when I first met you at church in Georgia."

After being in a fashion show to raise money for the Stuart Literacy Organization, I was hired by a local modeling agency to do some tearoom modeling. With that experience, I helped the literacy organization put on fashion shows that became a big yearly event. The shows helped the literacy group raise a lot of money. It was my first experience helping to raise thousands of dollars. That was rewarding as well as fun!

As the new director of volunteers at the church, I helped the staff by organizing the much-needed volunteers for this large congregation. With organized volunteers and three associate ministers, Joe was meeting the demands of this large member church.

One day, one of our associate ministers invited me to go along with him and a few members to visit a migrant camp a few miles out of Stuart. The camp was called Indian Town. The poor workers lived in small mobile homes without heat or air. They would be fine without heat in South Florida, but it was hot weather most of the year, and I saw babies placed on the floor on blankets without even a fan to keep them cool. The trailers were hot, and I saw some babies panting to breathe.

With my description about the need for fans written up in our church newsletter, we collected used fans and money for new fans for a lot of those people in Indian Town. We also collected other items that the people could use.

Our Stuart church was a membership blessed with a comfortable lifestyle and lovely homes, many on the beautiful rivers that surrounded the city. People who are blessed with so much should not be able to sleep conscience-free at night when little babies in a nearby neighborhood are in need of a fan. I watched the Indian Town project grow and grow until each week we had a room full of household items and clothes to take to Indian Town. One of our members, who owns a truck, volunteered to deliver the items each week. Most of all, I was thankful for the response of donated electric fans for the homes.

Our little cabin at Lake Junaluska, North Carolina, was a special retreat. It was a homey little two-bedroom house. We stayed there for a whole month away from the busy life in Stuart. The church had been left in the care of Dale Locke, Joe's talented associate. Joe needed the rest, but most of all, he enjoyed the big, shady trees that he missed not having in South Florida.

We had built our mountain cabin while at Lake Wales and had enjoyed many summer vacations there, watching our sons grow up. Junaluska was a safe place where Mark and Luke had been free to explore the neighborhood on their own. They played tennis with friends, fished in the nearby streams, or went swimming in the Methodist retreat center's pool.

One morning, the neighbors in the cottage above our cottage walked down to greet us. "You all must have been having a party last night," they said, hinting that they had heard a lot of extra noise and laughter.

"No, that was just us and our neighbors, the Harrisons. I know we were loud, laughing and telling jokes and singing old gospel songs. Ray and Rose have the cottage next to our cottage. Ray is also a Florida Conference minister, and we've been close friends for years," Joe explained.

"To tell you the truth, we thought you all were some renters down here DRUNK! But we're glad to know ministers and their wives can kick back and have fun like that."

Smiling, Joe said, "Wait until we get the rest of our gang up here. We've just begun."

After that, the cottage neighbors invited us and the other ministers and wives to their parties. Lots of summer fun was enjoyed by all!

By fall, the First United Methodist Church of Stuart became very busy again with extra activity. The Northern crowd, which usually stayed six months or longer, was migrating back South. By October, the church was overflowing. We had some very nice and sophisticated people in this church.

A new minister in Leesburg was enjoying the fruits of Joe's labor. He didn't need to have three services to accommodate the crowds. The new sanctuary was large enough to drop back to having only two services. In Stuart, Joe was back to straining his voice with three services of preaching and singing on Sunday mornings.

One Sunday morning, some out-of-town relatives were coming to visit, and they were arriving in time to join us at the eleven o'clock church service. When they got near the church, they saw police officers directing traffic off Kanner Highway. It looked like a traffic jam! There were cars everywhere, trying to get by each other as others were turning into the church parking lot. They had to wait several minutes before they could turn into the lot.

"Oh my God, there must be a terrible accident in front of Joe's church," one of the relatives said to the others in the car.

They didn't know that was the scene in front of Stuart First United Methodist Church every Sunday morning. The police were off-duty police officers hired by the church to direct the extra traffic. Also, the church had volunteers helping park all the cars in the front and side parking lots. I parked in the rear parking lot where there was less traffic. This was where the established members had parked for years, and I joined them. Sunday mornings were extra busy at Stuart First United Methodist Church!

Since Joe was busy with three services, he was not able to visit any of the Sunday school classes and see how they were doing. This was where the church had had some conflict before Joe was appointed. I visited all the adult Sunday school classes and the children's department. Children's classes were like those almost everywhere that used the Methodist Church literature. But the adult classes had a different style.

One class was an average, conservative group that used the Methodist Cokesbury literature for their lessons. Most of the members of this class were easygoing, relaxed-acting people who had probably grown up in a church. They didn't do any dramatic hand waving toward heaven during prayer time or have any heated debates over the points in their lessons. They just seemed to enjoy one another. And they had a lot of socials in their homes, always inviting their minister and his wife to be a part of their parties. Joe and I especially enjoyed watching the boat show each Christmas season with the members of this Sunday school class.

Another adult class was a very liberal class. There were lawyers, doctors, teachers, and other professionals in this class. There was a lot of discussion as well as debate and different opinions in this group. They discussed such books as *When Bad Things Happen to Good People.*

One doctor in the class seemed to enjoy shaking up another doctor's wife with such remarks as "I don't think I even believe in God anymore." One Sunday, she left the class crying. Later, he tried to test his minister's wife with one of his remarks but found out she couldn't be shaken. My college course in philosophy helped me understand different questions about beliefs and faith. I could easily join the debates. I enjoyed this class!

The largest adult Sunday school class had about three hundred people, and they met in the fellowship hall. When I visited this class, I sat in the back row, trying to be as inconspicuous as possible. This was a charismatic group, some waving their hands when their leader made a statement and some speaking in tongues during prayer time. This group certainly walked to the beat of a different drummer. I just didn't walk to their beat. When in their class, I felt like a spectator and a little guilty that I was observing them. But there were some very loving people in this class, and they were very supportive of my husband. This class was not all bad; they did a lot of good mission projects. They even had their own missionary in Africa.

One of my best friends was in the charismatic class. One day, as we were sitting on the beach, sunning and talking, I asked her, "Maureen, what made you choose your Sunday school class?" I knew Maureen was not a charismatic type of Christian.

She answered my question, "When I first came here from South Carolina, I found some of the friendliest people in the church were in this class. They invited me to their class, and I've stayed because it wasn't filled with Yankees like some of the other classes. I just don't have much in common with all these Northern people. That is why I enjoy being with you so much. You're Southern."

I thought to myself, *My friend is prejudiced. She might not like me if I wasn't from Georgia.*

Joe and I accepted and loved lots of people, and it didn't matter if they were from the North, South, or another country. I loved Maureen anyway. I didn't just throw a friend in the ocean because she didn't agree with my whole philosophy of life.

Later, the unbelievable happened. Maureen, the beautiful widow, married a Yankee! It had been just a few months since Maureen had told me why she had chosen the Sunday school class. Now, Joe and I were dancing at the lovely couple's wedding. Love does change people.

Maureen said, "John is the sweetest man I've ever met!" After her wedding, Maureen joined John's Sunday school class, which was one of the conservative classes with people from the North as well as the South.

Joe accepted the people in the charismatic class, but he let them know that he was not charismatic. He didn't have the gift of speaking in tongues, and he didn't want it. But if they wanted to be baptized with immersion, he would baptize them in a member's swimming pool. Most Methodist baptisms are done with sprinkling in the church sanctuary. Joe had respect for the charismatic people, and they were very supportive and respectful of him and his ministry. The bishop later bragged to Joe, "I knew you could deal with this group better than any other minister in the conference, and that's why we needed you there!"

Joe felt like people should accept one another's differences in faith. He took this to different levels. Sometimes, a member would be marrying a Catholic or a person of the Jewish faith. Joe performed their weddings, along with a priest or a rabbi. Some of his Protestant minister friends would not perform someone's wedding if he or she were not a member of a particular church.

I remember hearing an attractive lady say to Joe at a church night supper, "Reverend Joe, I'm engaged to a nice Jewish fellow. Would you agree to be a part of our ceremony?"

"Sure. What's the date? I'll get you on my calendar." Then Joe pulled out his little black book.

Joe and the rabbi worked nicely together. They performed a beautiful wedding at the Breakers in Palm Beach.

The community concerts were held in our church. Our church was chosen because it could seat the large crowds. The concert leaders were also members of the church, so they expected our support. We were given free concert tickets and invited to the private parties after the concerts to meet the entertainers.

Joe and I had attended concerts in other places, but we had never had community concerts as part of our church program. This was a new adventure for us. We were often pictured in the *Martin County Arts* news that was included in the West Palm magazine. With my formal dresses and Joe in his tux, we looked like part of the South Florida social life in those pictures.

You can dress up a country boy from Georgia, but you can't take the country out of his taste! This was the case when Joe had to sit miserably on the front row, pretending to enjoy a *classical guitar concert*! He thought they would play at least one or two pieces that he would recognize. To him, it was awful! That night, I had to attend the concert party alone because I was one of the hostesses. He went home and said, "Let someone else tell them, 'Great concert!'" Later, some of his friends laughed as he complained about his miserable evening at that concert.

There were many other concerts that Joe and I enjoyed. Roger Williams and Joe became buddies. He visited Stuart about once a year and became one of our favorites. Joe enjoyed playing piano by ear, and to hear Roger Williams play the piano in his church was special.

One morning before his evening concert, Roger Williams was practicing in the sanctuary as we walked by the open side door. We had left the office building on our way to lunch.

"Hey, Joe and Gloria, what are you guys up to?" Williams asked.

"I'm taking Gloria out to lunch, it's her birthday. Then, tonight we'll be at your concert!"

"Well, stop and let's sing 'Happy Birthday' to Gloria!" Williams played the piano, and he and Joe sang "Happy Birthday" to me. With appreciation, I kissed them both on the cheek. Not everyone had the special treat of a Roger Williams giving them a private mini birthday concert.

"Guess who's coming to our church in December? Your childhood singing idol, Pat Boone. And he wants our choir to do backup music for his concert."

Joe knew Pat Boone had been my teenage idol. When other teenyboppers were screaming over Elvis Presley, I would say, "I like Pat Boone's music better."

"Pat Boone is coming to our church!" I said. "That's special, and I'll get to sing backup music for my teenage idol. It's neat that he wants our choir to sing the backup music." I knew our talented choir director, Ralph, would have us well prepared.

December came, and so did the grandchildren. Mark and Martha brought Katie and Jay Hudson to the concert. During the concert, three-year-old Jay Hudson was sitting on his granddaddy's lap, and he kept pointing out to his parents that Gigi was up front singing. My little grandson made me realize who my special idol was now, and it wasn't any singer or movie star.

After the concert, Joe kept saying, "Gloria, we're going to be late for the dinner!"

A grandson was demanding his Gigi's attention. He wanted good night kisses. And I was not going to neglect those precious moments even for my teenage idol.

As we entered the door, we saw that Pat Boone, the arts center president, and her husband had already been seated. We knew that the arts center president had honored Pat Boone's request to keep the evening low-key, with only a dinner and maybe a couple or two to help fill up the table after the concert. Apparently, he had his fill of large parties.

We had been invited because the president of the arts center knew that Joe and I could be depended on for good table conversation. Joe was never at a loss for words and stories, neither was Pat Boone; he had some interesting stories too.

As we walked through the door, Joe whispered to me, "I told you we were going to be late."

Before we reached the table, Pat Boone and the group stood up to greet us. I was impressed. Later, I told Joe that we probably would have been expected to stand up for Pat Boone coming to the table if we hadn't been late, and being late let me not have to act like a celebrity's groupie.

It was an enjoyable evening. Pat Boone was an interesting and delightful person. He seemed to be a good family man and a loyal husband, as well as a man with a sincere faith.

Once a year, Joe had a special service called All States Day. This is an interesting church service since there are people from different states and countries in Florida. Some are retired and live in Florida six months or less and go back to homes up North during the warmer months. Joe started this special celebration while in Lake Wales since there were more winter visitors there than he had in former smaller churches. For this celebration, the church was decorated with all the state flags around the sanctuary as well as the usual large American and Christian flags.

Before the sermon, each state was recognized, and people stood and were counted for their state. It was like an enjoyable competition because everyone was interested in how many and who was from their state. Most people stood up for the state where they were born. It was surprising that Florida seldom had the highest number.

Georgia won sometimes. One Sunday in Stuart, on All States Day, every state in the union, as well as five countries, was represented.

"I think a trip to Alaska would be fun!" I said, encouraging Joe to accept the invitation from our friends, the Tindells, to cover their church work in Anchorage while they would be on a month's vacation in Europe. We could stay in their mountain home, which overlooked the city of Anchorage.

"I'll take my vacation time, and we'll fly to Alaska." Joe agreed after thinking it over.

Joe and I arrived in Anchorage on the night of the midnight sun. The sun didn't set until midnight, then after a little dusk light, the sun came back up. July was a month of sunlight with no dark nights in Anchorage, Alaska!

The lifestyle and the church work in the First United Methodist Church of Anchorage seemed slow and laid – back compared to Florida. The people were enjoying their long, relaxed summer days. People could be seen on the golf courses at ten and eleven o'clock at night. Young people were out playing softball and tennis.

This slow lifestyle was great, giving Joe and me lots of free time. We took day trips and were able to see the sights like regular tourists.

I told relatives on the phone, "Everyone should take a camera to Alaska because the landscape in Alaska is a photographer's paradise! The mountains are bigger and higher, the flowers are brighter, the lakes and streams are fresh and clear, and the animals are everywhere."

Both of us had a hard time adjusting to twenty-four-hour light! I just put on my little pink satin blinders and slept five or six hours. At first, Joe stayed up watching television or reading most of the night. Finally, I found him a pair of eye covers, and he got some sleep.

The church had two Sunday services, one at eight-thirty and the regular eleven o'clock service. The people were friendly and made us feel welcome. During the month of July, Joe did not have a funeral or a wedding. That was certainly different from his Florida work schedule. Some people think ministers only work on Sundays. In Alaska during the month of July, that was almost true. Joe did make a few visits with people in the hospital. He took prepared sermons that he had written in Stuart, so he didn't have to work on sermons. That gave us more leisure time to visit parks, glaciers, and take the long train ride to other parts of Alaska.

We had a great time in Alaska in spite of less sleep. The never-ending sunlight made the month seem like a year. Joe was ready to kiss the ground when our plane landed back in Atlanta, Georgia. My sister Lois and her husband, Doug, welcomed us back to Georgia. A few hours later, Grandmother Grace and our little dog, Rambo, welcomed us back to Moultrie. After a short visit with family and a sharing of my many pictures of the Alaskan scenery, we drove back to Stuart, ready to face our busy life there.

After seeing many of our friends and members travel pictures, we knew better than to share those pictures with other people. Boring! Only a mother can love you enough to enjoy your travel pictures. And maybe a sister or a brother can appreciate grandchildren's pictures. After seeing someone's baby pictures, how many people put on an actor's voice when saying, "Oh, what a beautiful baby!"

It was one of those weeks in Stuart when Joe had five funerals scheduled. *Did people really come to Florida to die in the sun?* we wondered. Of course, the associates helped with the funerals to lighten Joe's load. Still, he needed to find time to comfort each family. A call or visit from the senior pastor was always expected and appreciated.

"Joe, what am I going to say?" the part-time, older associate asked in his most serious mood. "His mother is such a nice lady."

The associate was referring to the funeral of a middle-aged man who had been in a motorcycle accident and was killed. The pastors knew the man's mother but had not known the man himself. He was not a church member.

The associate continued describing the situation to Joe. "Last night, his buddies visited the funeral home, and they put a beer can in the casket by his hand. They were all dressed in black leather. Then there's his well-dressed mother and her friends. I know what to say for the mother and friends, but I've never had a motorcycle crowd for a funeral. What do I say?"

Joe saw the humor in the situation. "Oh, Carl, just read John 3:16 and say *voroom-voroom* [motorcycle sound], then a few more words and *voroom-voroom-voroom!*"

Of course, Reverend Carl laughed and said, "Joe, I can just see myself in the middle of a serious service thinking of your advice."

Reverend Carl did a fine job for the funeral service in spite of Joe's "advice."

A group in our church decided to go with a district group of people to help a little Methodist Church in the Dominican Republic. It was a short-term mission trip. They would help build a fellowship hall. They asked me if I wanted to go with them. At first, I didn't think I would be very good helping them with a building project. But they convinced me that there were other things that needed doing, like helping with the meals, being the group's photographer, and giving devotions at the planned evening church services.

I joined the group and had a different kind of religious work experience. I had seen poverty in America but never like the poverty in this country. There were little children begging on the streets, and every day, someone came to the minister's parsonage begging for food. The minister's wife had little bags of food prepared to hand out each day. The water was not fit to drink, and each day, a water delivery truck came by the house selling water. We would be getting ready to go to the church, and the electricity would go off. Almost every day the electricity was down for several hours. The night that I was giving my speech at the church, the electricity went off, and I had to read my notes by the light of a lamp.

The day that the group was taking a long bus ride into the hills to visit an orphanage, I was disappointed that I could not go because I had brought a suitcase full of gifts for children. The long ride over bumpy, rough, unpaved roads was not something my back could tolerate. I sent my gifts for the children with the group, and I stayed at the parsonage and went shopping at the market with the minister's married daughter. That was an experience in itself!

It certainly wasn't like my Publix supermarket in Stuart. The fruit and vegetables were displayed in wooden boxes, and the meat was hung in large uncut pieces. The people were friendly, speaking to me in Spanish like I was one of them. When I wasn't with our group from America, I seemed to fit right in with my Florida suntan and dark hair and brown eyes. The Dominican people came in all shades of skin. Some were light brown, some a darker shade of brown, and some were black.

When the people spoke to me in Spanish, I spoke back and loved seeing the expression on their faces when they realized my accent was different. My few weeks of studying the language before the trip made my speaking in Spanish limited, and I wondered how weird my accent must sound. But I got by and could get my basic needs met at the parsonage with the minister's wife who didn't speak a word of English.

It was an interesting two weeks, and I loved getting some wonderful snapshots. It was an extra-special trip for me because after my skiing accident that injured my back, I never thought I could be strong enough to take a mission trip.

Our family met in Moultrie to have Thanksgiving with Joe's parents. Joe and I arrived a few days early. We needed to help Mother Grace with the dinner preparations. We bought homemade cakes from a Catholic church's bake sale down the street from Joe's parents' home. Mother Grace still insisted that she make her own pumpkin and pecan pies.

Mark and Luke's families arrived on Thanksgiving morning. With the arrival of grandchildren, there was a lot of excitement! A delicious Thanksgiving dinner was enjoyed by all. Granddaddy Hubert was usually the life of the party, but he was unusually quiet this Thanksgiving. Everyone knew he wasn't feeling well.

Mark and Martha decided to take the children to the farm and spend the night there so the house would be quieter for Granddaddy Hubert. They always had fun at the farm and the island camp house. The short boat ride to the little island was an exciting adventure for the children.

Joe and I had to leave on the Saturday after Thanksgiving so Joe could be in the pulpit on Sunday. As we were driving back to Florida, Joe said, "Dad's heart seems to be giving him some problems again. He didn't seem to feel good at all. Did you notice how little he ate?"

"Yes, I noticed, and he always enjoyed your mother's cornbread dressing and would repeat several times how good the dressing was. This Thanksgiving, he didn't even mention the dressing."

Joe and I went to bed early that night, tired from the long trip back to Stuart.

Early the next morning, Luke called. "Granddaddy had a heart attack this morning, and he's gone. I tried to save him, but he didn't respond."

"We'll be on our way back to Moultrie as soon as I get the associate minister, Dale, to take care of the church services. Tell Mother we're on our way back," Joe told Luke.

It isn't easy for anyone to lose a parent, no matter the age. Joe expressed his feelings as we drove back to Georgia. "I'm glad Dad didn't suffer with a long illness, and I'm real thankful he didn't have to be bedridden in a nursing home. There are some things that are worse than death."

"He was a good father, and he gave us a lot of joy with his wild sense of humor. We'll all miss him," I said, patting Joe's hand. Joe often comforted the grieving, and now it was my time to try and comfort him. But that was hard to do because his dad had become like a father to me too.

We discussed how wonderful it was that Joe's parents had celebrated their fiftieth wedding anniversary. We were glad we had the nice anniversary party for them. *How do people adjust not having a mate after living together for more than fifty years?* we wondered.

After the funeral, it was hard leaving Mother Grace all alone in that big house in Moultrie. She bravely said, "I'll be okay."

Back in Stuart, one of our church members was having a party for a visiting astronaut. Joe and I were invited to this special occasion. It was awesome meeting one of the few men who had been to the moon. Everyone gathered in the large living room to talk and visit with him and his wife. One of the questions asked was "Did you have a spiritual moment while out in space?"

"Yes, looking back at the Earth and seeing how small it looks from the moon makes one have a special spiritual feeling, but I didn't see any angels or anything like that," he answered. (To protect his family's privacy, the astronaut's name is not mentioned here.)

During the evening, I had the opportunity to chat with the astronaut's wife. I will not forget the comment she made about being married to a famous man. What she said may be true for a lot of successful people and their families.

She said, "He gave most of his life preparing for that trip to the moon. And his family had to do without a father and a husband much of the time. While he was in training, my parents helped me raise our children. *Fame has a price.*"

Meeting some of the rich and famous gave me a better understanding of people. Everyone needs love and understanding. No matter the person's standing in life, they have their sorrows as well as their joys. Just because they are well-known doesn't make them exempt from the ups and downs that each of us face in life. Of course, the movie magazines make the lives of stars look like perfection, with few of the cares of average folk. But sometimes, average folk live much better lives than some of these so-called stars. For every movie star, there are hundreds of women more beautiful and men more handsome. And for every famous guy, there are thousands of people as brilliant without the fame. Some use their fame to help others and make the world a better place while others live in self-centered circles, looking for happiness and fortune in all the wrong places.

I was sleeping when I heard a knock on my bedroom window. I woke up frightened and wondering, *Is someone trying to break my window?* The curtains were drawn, and I couldn't see. Again, I heard the urgent knock. I jumped out of bed and ran down the hall to peep out the sliding glass back door. It was Joe, and he was still knocking on the window. I knew he had planned to go early to the gym, but why was he back knocking on our bedroom window?

He'd better not kid me this way! I thought. Then I saw the look on his face, and it was strange. I opened the sliding door.

"Joe, what's wrong?"

"Uh, uh, uh," Joe tried to tell me something.

"Joe, have you seen a terrible accident or something?"

Then I realized that he couldn't talk. He seemed to be in shock! *Maybe he's had a stroke!* I thought.

After getting him through the door, I ran to the phone and called the doctor. The neurologist was a member of our church, and I knew he would meet us at the hospital.

He said, "Bring Joe to the emergency room, and I'll meet you there."

To get Joe oriented enough to get him in the car and to the hospital was a task in itself.

In the emergency room, the doctor gave Joe a quick test, and it showed that he'd had a TIA (transient ischemic attack). This type of stroke is an attack that usually lasts for only a few minutes and is a warning signal that a sufficient supply of blood is not reaching part of the brain.

Joe had never been in the hospital in his life, and he didn't find it a welcome experience. He understood what the doctor was saying, but he could not put his thoughts back into words.

The doctor said, "His speech will slowly come back, starting in a few hours, but he'll need to stay in the hospital overnight."

The next morning, Joe was able to explain what happened while he was at the gym. He was sitting in the sauna when he felt like he was going to faint. He got out of the sauna, sat in a chair for a few minutes, and then thought he'd better drive home and go back to bed. He didn't know how he drove home. When he got to the garage, he found it strange that he couldn't remember how to work the automatic garage door. That was the reason he walked to the backyard and knocked on the bedroom window. He just wanted to go to bed!

After Joe got home from the hospital, he called his good friend Lee Pearson at the Florida Methodist Enrichment Center. With a description of his hospital experience, he told Lee how he comforted himself during the period that he couldn't talk.

"Lee, I just told myself I'll go to the life enrichment center and mow grass. My friend Lee will give me that job."

"Hell, you think I would have hired you?" Lee jokingly retorted. And they continued laughing and talking. Two ministers with the same unholy sense of humor!

Joe was back in the pulpit the next Sunday after the TIA. But the attack got his attention. He agreed with me that the pressures of the busy lifestyle and large congregation might be too much stress for his health. He needed more than a vacation. He needed to ask the bishop for a smaller appointment and downsize a bit.

There were some wonderful people in the Stuart church. We had made some great friends. But a change was needed. The district superintendent and the bishop understood, and the move was set for the next June.

Before moving, Joe couldn't resist making light of his move to the congregation. He told them one Sunday morning, "I'm moving to Ocala, horse racing country.

Now if you hear of a horse named Holy Joe, bet on him! That's what I'll be naming my race horse."

We had both celebrated our fiftieth birthdays while in Stuart. We now had five grandchildren: Katie, Whitney, Jay Hudson, Amy, and David. Someday, Claire and Meredith would join the gang, and we would have a total of seven grands! We had definitely aged while in Stuart.

As usual, the church members gave a great going-away dinner party. Joe and I shook hands and gave hugs, telling everyone goodbye.

No matter how large the congregation, some of the people will remain in our hearts forever. They may have shared some special experience that could never be forgotten, such as a wedding, a baptism, or the comforting words said at the funeral of their mate. Some of the special people in the Stuart church were the Evans, the Farrows, the Arnolds, the Blounts, the Dalys, the Bolands, the Evans, the Bozones, the Gudemans, the Hartmans, the Herndons, the Joneses, the Lockes, the Raynors, the Schmidts, the Sentells, the Tiltons, and the Wrights, as well as all the special staff who helped make a large church run smoothly.

Moving from Stuart was the first time that I didn't cry about moving because going back to Central Florida was like going home. We would have trees again, large oak trees with deep roots, just like some of the people. Our grown sons, daughters-in-law, and grandchildren were there! And we would be getting nearer to Georgia where aging parents needed more visits. Joe's mother and my mother were always begging for more and longer visits.

While going over the long, high bridge out of Stuart, I was singing, "So long, it's been good to know you, what a long time since I've been home, and I've got to be drifting along!"

Joe was driving his car, and I was following in my car. I knew he was happy about this move. It's always better to be happy than to feel disappointed about a move.

OCALA, FLORIDA: 1991-1994

AT FIRST GLANCE from the street, one might think the First United Methodist Church of Ocala is a Catholic church. We admired the beautiful statue of Christ with outstretched arms at the front of the sanctuary. The buildings around the sanctuary were surrounded with lovely live oaks decorated with hanging moss. The green lawns were thick and immaculate. There was a look of stability and history. Central Florida had more of this stable look than South Florida.

With such a large church plant, it didn't look like Joe was sizing down. The membership was a few hundred less than the Stuart church and the salary much less. We were making some adjustments in our lifestyle, but we knew some things were more important than money, such as health and more time for family.

The parsonage was a lovely brick home. It was furnished with some very nice traditional furniture. But like most parsonages, it needed some updating. My longtime friend Sally Howell would help me. She and her husband, Bill, had been members of the Lake Wales church. They had moved to Ocala years ago and were again members of our church. Sally had helped me decorate and update the Lake Wales parsonage. She was just the person I needed to help with the Ocala parsonage.

I often said, "Sally has a doctoral degree in shopping. She knows where everything can be found on a shopping list."

When we finished the decorating job, the house was ready for entertaining. We had fun updating and decorating another parsonage together.

Soon after moving to Ocala, the church members wanted a new family life center. This gave Joe another building program, which he always enjoyed. He organized a building committee made of people who were great to work with. Life was a little more relaxed than in South Florida, but there was much work to be done at this church too.

It didn't take long for Joe to find one of the horse farm owners. They were everywhere around Ocala. Beautiful horse farms! While visiting one of the church members, Joe said, "I told them in Stuart that I was going to have a horse in Ocala with the name Holy Joe."

"That sounds like a winner! Let me show you my new colt that was born last night. He needs a good name. We'll name him Holy Joe."

Every week or so, Joe rode out to the horse farm and watched Holy Joe in training. He watched him off and on for a couple of years. Joe couldn't wait to see him on the race track.

Holy Joe turned out to be the laziest horse in Ocala. He never won any races. But he was beautiful.

The Ocala church had a television ministry. Every Sunday, at the beginning of the service, Joe greeted the people watching on TV. After the greeting, he forgot all about them and spoke directly to his congregation.

Joe never desired a television ministry. Most television evangelist just seemed phony to him. He desired his ministry to be genuine. He preached down-to-earth sermons, sprinkled with encouragement about facing the ups and downs of daily living. Hellfire or streets of milk and honey or "Send us your money, and we'll guarantee you will be healed" were not his type of ministry. Everyone has their own vision of heaven or hell, and Joe didn't mess with those visions.

One Monday morning, the church secretary said, "Joe, the church's television ratings have been made."

"Really? I wonder how they do that. Well, how did we rate?" he asked.

"The sermon time got the same rating as the Crystal Cathedral. But the children's story [with George] got the highest rating of the morning, more than the Crystal Cathedral hour or your sermon time."

"You mean a monkey has upstaged my sermons. That's amazing!"

A five-year-old little girl with lovely red hair had picked on George for several Sundays. She poked at his eyes, pulled his tail, and stuck her finger in his mouth. Quietly, Joe gave George permission to put a stop to her mischievous conduct.

An older lady described what she saw on television. "Reverend Smith, I was sick with a little bug Sunday and saw the church service on television. That was the cutest thing when George was pinched, and he quickly turned and bit that little girl's finger. You should have seen the shocked expression on her face. The cameraman did a close up of her, and it was priceless! Then you went right on with the story like nothing had happened."

Joe had heard the old saying growing up, "If people live long enough, they will go through a second childhood." Like children, the folks at the nursing home seemed like they'd rather have a visit from George, the toy monkey, than their pastor.

"Please, bring George to see us!" they begged.

Joe gave in, and soon he always had George on his arm as he entered the Ocala Nursing Home. At first, the nursing home staff looked at him a bit oddly, like *he* was the one in his second childhood. Then they saw how happy the toy monkey made the residents as it kissed the ladies and shook hands with the men.

"I watch him on television every Sunday. I like the stories he helps you tell the children," a lady in a wheelchair commented.

Soon, the staff and nurses were smiling and saying, "Bring him back soon, Reverend Smith. George makes their day."

The veterinarians in town had a special project that I was interested in. They would check out a pet and make sure he was acceptable for visiting older people in nursing homes. Our little eight-pound white toy poodle, Rambo, was perfect for this project. He loved people and was a sweet, beautiful, gentle pet. It seemed that I always found a different type of ministry or activity in each new town that we lived in. This was a rewarding project because I could share my precious pet with people who needed some special, unconditional love.

Many of the nursing home patients were reminded of their younger days when they'd had pets of their own. It seemed a treat just to touch Rambo's soft fur and pet his small head. Men and women would tell me their dog stories with a sparkle in their eyes as they reminisced. Some just smiled and patted his head.

One Sunday, Rambo was shared at the church for the children's story. Some of the nursing home people enjoyed seeing him that morning on the church's television hour. Joe told how Rambo was a hero. He saved us from a robber at the grandparents' home in Moultrie. The robber was stealing things out of the garage at night when everyone was there for Thanksgiving. The grandbabies were sleeping there too, and Rambo knew he had lots of work to do that night protecting them. He heard a noise outside and woke up his masters because he wanted to go outside to check things out. When he saw it was a robber, he barked as loud as he could and chased the robber down the street. We yelled, "Rambo, come back!" Hearing that big name, the robber probably thought he was a big dog. After that appearance on television, Rambo was a big hero to his nursing home friends too.

When the grandchildren visited, Joe and I took them to Mr. Guy's miniature horse farm. They rode in a cute little buggy pulled by Buck. Rambo liked to ride in the buggy with them too. And they had rides on the backs of Sugar, Princess, and Baby. They thought the little horses were the cutest and sweetest little creatures in the whole world!

I loved the little horses too. Mr. Guy heard me say to Joe, "We've got to buy some miniature horses for our farm in Georgia when we retire!"

"I'll be ready to sell you mine by then," Mr. Guy said. "I'm sure someday this will be too much work for this old retired man."

One night, Mr. Guy called about midnight saying, "Do you still want to see Sugar give birth? Her little colt will arrive soon."

"Sure, we'll drive out!" We dressed, and I grabbed my camera. Out the door, we hurried to Mr. Guy's farm.

By the time we reached Mr. Guy's barn, the precious little colt had been born. "Oh, how I wish the grandchildren could see this!" I was fascinated with the baby colt as I snapped pictures for the grandchildren.

"Now, I'll help him up on his wobbly legs to nurse." Mr. Guy was a proud helper for the little mother horse.

The next morning, I couldn't wait to call the grandchildren. I told them, "The little horse named Sugar had a baby colt. Mr. Guy named the baby colt Glory."

Joe and I enjoyed Silver Springs in Ocala. We had season tickets, so many Sunday afternoon walks were taken at the springs. For years, it had been one of Florida's favorite tourist attractions. After tiring from a walk, we would sit in a swing on the lovely grounds and watch the people, acting like we owned the place. When the grandchildren visited, we took them riding on the glass-bottom boats, viewing the large fish at the springs. We loved the Jungle Cruise! There were interesting animals to see while cruising by the riverbanks.

Silver Springs had some nice outdoor concerts with well-known entertainers, and we enjoyed attending some of these special concerts. Christmas season was another special time when we visited Silver Springs at night. Caroling was the entertainment, shops were open, and lovely candles lighted all the winding paths at beautiful Silver Springs.

While in Ocala, I felt strong enough to start taking more college courses again. I now felt that I was too old to have a career in teaching, so I chose psychology and counseling as my new degree goal. I had had a lot of practical experience counseling people who came to me with their problems, especially when Joe wasn't available or they just wanted a woman's view of the situation. A lot of people with illness or chronic pain had come to me for encouragement. This made my new studies much easier than they would have been for me in my younger years, without those years of practical experience.

Like all the past church appointments, the Ocala First United Methodist Church had more than enough to keep a minister busy. There were sermons to write, weddings, funerals, suppers, and parties, as well as community events.

I also had meetings, events, choir rehearsals, and concerts to attend. My life was still busy, but not as busy as Stuart, so that gave me extra time to work on my studies.

And there were visits with the grandchildren. Luke and Karen both worked in Leesburg, so when the babies were sick, I made the hour trip to care for my sick grandbaby while the parents worked.

While we were in Ocala, we heard the sad news about our first Florida appointment, the Redland church in Homestead. It had stood many hurricanes, but finally one blew it down. Like a mother always remembers her firstborn, we would always remember the little white church building that looked like a little church in the wildwood, surrounded by palm trees and papaya groves. When we heard the news, it was like part of ourselves had been blown away with it.

The member's letter said, "In the picture you can see only the wooden cross stands high and strong in the midst of the rubble. Thank God, all our friends are safe. But the reports of the area are very sad. Many people lost loved ones and the city looks like a boom destroyed it. Those beautiful Royal Palms that lined the main street were blown down, too."

In the Florida Methodist Conference, the bishop's office is in Lakeland, Florida. The churches in the state are in districts with a district superintendent. The bishop appoints district superintendents to help make appointments for all the churches in the state. They take care of a lot of church-related business.

Joe had been in Ocala only three years when the bishop called, asking him to accept an appointment as district superintendent of the Gainesville district.

Joe reluctantly accepted the bishop's appointment. "Bishop, all I've ever wanted to be is a pastor, but if this is where the conference needs me, I'll go."

"Now, you will have the opportunity to be a pastor to other pastors and their families with this appointment," his new bishop encouraged him.

Before hanging up the phone, the bishop said, "By the way, Joe, this means you have to be at all the annual conference meetings. You can no longer go fishing before the week is over."

"How did you know I've been guilty of doing that for years, Bishop?"

"Your friends talk!" The bishop chuckled as they ended the conversation.

Joe called me from the church office to tell me the news. Since we had only been in Ocala for three years, packing for another move was the least of my plans for the coming year. I had hoped to finish up my degree in psychology and family counseling. But with colleges and the university in Gainesville, I should be able to finish my last few courses.

Joe said, "At least this should be our last move before retirement."

I told him, "I think I'll like your new appointment. We will be free to be with our family for Christmas and other holidays. We have always had to share Christmas and Easter with our churches."

"That's right," Joe agreed. "The pastors will take care of Christmas and Easter in their churches, and they certainly will not need a district superintendent at these times."

"We can be with our mothers and our children for holidays and some weekends. That will be great. Besides, I'll have a husband sitting with me at church instead of always in the pulpit."

I was excited. And Joe couldn't help but agree that this may be a good appointment after all. This would be our last appointment to "bloom where we are appointed."

GAINESVILLE, FLORIDA: 1994-2000

A FTER MOVING INTO the Gainesville district parsonage, the ministers gave us a welcome party. All the pastors and their mates were present. Getting to meet a group of pastors is like getting to know any other group of people. There are the young, the old, the smart, and the lazy ones, as well as the exciting ones and the reserved ones.

In 1994, there were seventy-three churches in the Gainesville district. Joe made it his goal to visit and meet with the leaders of all seventy-three churches each year. He listened to their problems and their joys.

He also had a private conference once a year with each pastor to discuss moving to another appointment or staying with their present church appointment.

If a pastor was moving to a place that he was excited about, he gave Joe credit for helping the bishop make his appointment. Joe shared that excitement. But it worked the opposite way too. If a pastor was not happy with his appointment, he might blame his district superintendent or the bishop. Of course, Joe understood this reaction. He had experienced the ups and downs of new appointments.

With the help of Ann Green, who was a very capable secretary, Joe's reports from each church were organized, typed, and sent to the bishop's office in Lakeland, Florida. The district office was more like a business office than like a local church office.

When the bishop called for the district superintendents to come for a retreat meeting, the mates were also invited. The retreats were held in some very nice locations. While the meetings were in session, the mates went shopping or sightseeing. Later, everyone met again for dinner. This was a time of fellowship and the opportunity to develop close friendships and support for one another. Often we were in places that gave our group VIP treatment. There was a lot of special respect for a bishop and his cabinet.

Was it lonely at the top? It certainly was not the same personal touch that a pastor has with his own congregation. Joe missed the local pastorate. But he kept his sense of humor and shared it with his fellow ministers and the other district superintendents as well as the bishop.

At one of the cabinet meetings, Joe ended up with the sheet that had all the ministers of the Miami district. No one liked getting that list because many of the pastors were Spanish, and the names were difficult to pronounce. It was easier to read the names of the Orlando district or the Tallahassee district.

When it came time for Joe to read his list, he confidently called out each Spanish name in a put-on accent with a weird enunciation. He did this to the names he knew how to pronounce correctly as well as the ones he didn't know. By the time he got through the Miami list, he had the bishop and the rest of the cabinet members cracked up with laughter. It was hard for the bishop's cabinet to be stuffy around Joe.

As the mate of a district superintendent, I had some responsibilities that came along with the position. The ministers' mates, most of them women, still looked to the superintendent's wife as their mentor and leader. I had once-a-month meetings with the pastors' wives. And with the help of the wives, I organized and planned socials for the ministers and for the ministers' families, such as the yearly welcome parties, picnics, and the end-of-year socials.

Few professions require as much perfection as being a pastor. When a pastor practices unacceptable moral standards or commits a crime, he or she must be dismissed by the church. Joe had a couple of pastors who were unacceptable for the ministry. It was Joe's job as district superintendent to dismiss them from their positions. When an unacceptable person gets in the church as a pastor, it's like having a wolf in sheep's clothing.

Joe was thankful that most of his pastors practiced what they preached. Most pastors and their mates are fine, moral, outstanding people who give of themselves with lots of love to other people. They share people's sorrows as well as their joys.

Joe was in Lakeland at the bishop's office for one of his out-of-town meetings when I got a call from a minister's wife, and she was crying. "What's wrong, Helen?" I asked.

"Could you meet me at the mall? I need to talk! I've got a big problem," she said.

As we sat in a restaurant booth at the mall, this poor woman poured her heart out to me.

"My husband is one thing in the pulpit and another thing at home. Everyone thinks of him as this nice, good, holy fellow, but he comes home and treats me awful. He looks at pornography and compares my body to those bodies in the magazines. He tells me I need to get in shape. He also tries to keep me from visiting my relatives. He even held me down physically the other night when I tried to leave."

Wiping her eyes, she continued, "I need help. I want to leave and go home to my family."

Then Helen's cell phone rang. It was her husband calling. "Yes, I'm still at the mall. I'll be back soon."

She turned back to me. "See how he keeps checking on me."

After listening to her problem, I told her what I would do if I were in her situation. "Sunday morning, while he's busy at the church, I would quickly pack my car with my personal items. Then I would drive away to my family and not look back."

"Or I'll turn into a pillar of salt if I look back." She tried to smile.

"That's what I mean. Just be thankful that you do not have children in this situation," I added.

We hugged goodbye.

The next Sunday morning, Helen had a relative come over and help her pack her personal belongings. She drove away while her abusive husband was busy at the church.

When Joe came home from his meetings in Lakeland, he was shocked to learn of that pastor's secret conduct. The problem had to be dealt with immediately. After discussing the problem with the bishop, they agreed that the man must not be back in the pulpit another Sunday. With more investigation, they learned that he had been disciplined for improper conduct in another conference before moving to Florida. The proper steps were taken, and that minister could no longer serve in a Methodist church.

One of my last courses taken at St. Leo University was a course titled Religion and Personal Experience. While taking this course, I was able to look inward and think about my own personal religious faith. Ministers and their mates stay so busy encouraging others in the faith that they sometimes fail to strengthen their own faith. It is like the man who repairs and makes shoes but has no shoes for himself. The readings of others who had struggled with the questions of life and their own personal faith stimulated my own thoughts. I cannot answer for my husband or my children or my friends on their personal thoughts about their faith, but I can share mine.

I think life can sometimes be a lonely inward journey, and no one can travel that journey for you. There's an old gospel song that says, "You've got to walk this lonesome valley. You've got to walk it by yourself." Of course, you can choose to walk it with God, or you can walk it alone. I like to think of it as "Climb Every Mountain" and reach for your impossible dreams with God's help.

After reading some of the thoughts of William James in *The Sick Soul*, I thought how the church had helped to form my faith. First, the Presbyterian Church nurtured my childhood faith, and then, as a teenager, I joined the Methodist Church. At least I'm Methodist as my public self, but inside I feel very ecumenical. I like to be free to accept, like an eclectic, all good parts of different religious faiths. I feel fortunate that

I am part of a church that will allow me to have freedom of thoughts and actions so that I can accept what comforts my free spirit.

I think that my insights are certainly in agreement with the writings of William James. I've quoted him for years since I took a philosophy course in the early 1960s. It is my will to believe.

My life has gone from small churches in the "wildwoods" to large churches with high steeples. Still, inwardly, the special feelings and the special insights are what really count, no matter if they happen in a humble shack or in a big mansion or in the woods or alone in a beautiful garden. They are the same meaningful experiences!

I hope some of these experiences of my Christian walk trying to find a stronger faith in a higher power will help someone find a deeper faith. Each person has to find God for himself or herself. Read, seek, and you will find.

Just as Martin Luther experienced unhealthy minded sins and pains in his spiritual journey, I too have experienced some of these worries and frustrations about life, such as pain and suffering. *God, why do I have to brave this pain in my back? God, why do families have to be torn apart? God, why do wars continue when many people pray and want a peaceful world?* After reading about the spiritual struggles of others, it helps to put one's own spiritual journey in perspective.

Many years I had to retch over living down the "sins of the fathers" and trying to control the effects of that alcoholic in the family. It took a lot of maturing and prayers before I was freed from the sins of my earthly father.

This type of maturing leaves me feeling very thankful, yet humble, that God has granted me the opportunity to understand, see the light, and grow in my own spiritual journey. Some people go to their graves feeling their lives were ruined by the sins of the fathers or their own miserable sins and mistakes.

I believe God is the most ideal part of the universe of which we are a part. I think God can be a part of a person or a person can reject God. A godly person has a conscience and knows what is right and wrong. A person without God can be a very lonely, sad individual and can sometimes sink to being a social deviant type of person.

Of course, as a Christian, I accept the Bible as my holy book. And I can quote scripture like a good Baptist, which I'm not. But beginning in my childhood and on to adulthood, I noticed people and some "preachers" taking the Bible out of context as well as giving out poor and negative interpretations. I view the Bible from a historical point of view, but that doesn't make it less holy for me. With my personal view, I have no problem with some scientific studies conflicting with the Old Testament. I remember the Bible verse that says, "When I was a child, I thought as a child" (1 Cor. 13:11).

Just because my husband is a minister and I have taken Bible courses doesn't make me an authority on the Bible. I'll leave the authority of the scriptures up to the seminary professors. I'll continue to read about the great spiritual leaders like Mother Teresa. Even Martin Luther King Jr. learned noble actions for life from Gandhi. Still,

I think reading the thoughts and seeing the actions of some of the great minds of the past helps average folk find some insights for a better faith journey.

Viktor E. Frankl wrote *Man's Search for Meaning*. I place it up there among the best books I have ever read. He wrote, "If there is meaning in life at all, then there must be a meaning in suffering."

As Frankl says, the person who suffers can have the freedom of choice to either add a deeper meaning to his or her life or take the opposite approach and act like an animal with selfishness and a bitter spirit. Sometimes, an exceptionally difficult external situation gives a person the opportunity to grow inwardly, spiritually beyond himself or herself.

In my long struggles with pain and weak moments of despair, God gave me patience, hope, faith, and the will to find answers when it seemed even the medical community did not have all the right answers. I found that it takes the mental as well as the physical and the spiritual working together to overcome obstacles in life.

Frankl's writings helped me understand that a person can accept the challenge to suffer bravely, which gives meaning to life up to the last moment, literally to the end of life.

Just as joy, happiness, and peace is universal, so is suffering. Most people don't get through life without some suffering. Hopefully, it will be short or just a little taste, but having faith in God helps one to brave that negative part of life and find some meaning in it all.

To know that even the great spiritual leaders of the past had their moments of despair helped me feel better about my own questions of faith. Reaching for a higher and better relationship with God can be a lifelong journey. So maybe the Lord *ain't* finished with me yet. I have my songs to sing and my books to write.

It helps to take the wisdom of others like Francis of Assisi who wrote this passage:

> Lord, make me an instrument of your peace.
> Where there is injury, let me bring pardon;
> Where there is hatred, love,
> Where there is doubt, faith,
> Where there is despair, hope,
> Where there is darkness, light,
> Where there is sadness, joy,
> O Divine Master, grant that I may not seek so much
> To be consoled as to console,
> To be understood as to understand,
> To be loved as to love;
> For it is in giving that we receive,
> It is in pardoning that we are pardoned,
> And it is in dying that we are born to eternal life.

When some of us start out in life young and inexperienced, we think we might change the world. Long ago, I learned that I'm doing okay if I can just change my little corner of the world and help make it a better place.

When Joe was out of town for conference meetings in Lakeland, I was alone in Gainesville much of the time. I spent some of my time finishing my college degree, which I had always wanted to do. Several of my instructors at St. Leo University also taught at the University of Florida. I had finally got to a place in life where I could work on my degree goal.

I was taking my last course in psychology, which required an in-depth research paper as well as many hours of volunteer work for practical experience. I was working at a mental health center and an abuse center for women and children.

One afternoon at the mental health center, I assisted a health worker taking a group of people outside to play a game of lawn bowling. The game looked like so much fun, and I did the unthinkable. I threw the ball! It was a good roll, a very good roll for a weak back, and everyone cheered.

For years, I had protected my weak spine, but it only took a moment of forgetting my limitations, and I was in big, serious trouble. It was acute pain! A person can learn to manage chronic pain and not let it control his or her life, but acute pain cannot be tolerated for very long. It was weeks before the best specialist could be found to do what would be the fifth surgery on my back. Without the pressure taken off the spinal nerve, I could not have survived. I cannot go into the details of the discomfort because it is indescribable.

Having to drop my last course and again delay my goal of a degree was like having salt rubbed into the wound. At this point, I didn't feel that it was important any longer. I just wanted to get well enough to walk again.

Almost a year later, my psychology professor called and encouraged me to finish my last course of study. And I was given credit for my work at the abuse center for women and children.

Finally, I graduated with honors, and my sons and my grandchildren attended my graduation. What a trip!

After finishing my degree in psychology, I took a job with the local abuse center for women and children called Sexual Physical Abuse Resource Center (SPARC). In 1998, they surprised me at a banquet with the Super Star Award. I had given a lot of extra time and energy helping the abused women and children but did not expect or seek an award. With work, church activities, and lots of visits with family, my life was once again very full and joyful.

Life taught me that without winters, springs would not be so welcome, and without adversity, success would not be so rewarding.

At the University of Florida in Gainesville, there were the football games. There was extra excitement in town when the Gators were the national champions.

A few times, Joe viewed the games from the skybox with friends. That was a special treat! For most of the games, we watched them on television in the comfort of home.

One of my nieces, Alyson, was in college in Gainesville, so she and her friends were at the parsonage often for pizza and chili suppers. Also, five of our Lam children were in school at the university, and they made visits to our parsonage too. Thank goodness we still had a lively home after our sons were grown and had families of their own.

For years, Joe had known that he had a heart valve problem. Doctors had told him that he would someday need surgery to fix the valve. The problem was causing him to tire easily. He went to the office in the mornings, took a long nap after lunch, and he still complained of feeling tired. The long nap made it possible for him to work evenings as he usually had a district meeting at one of the churches.

We took walks around the neighborhood or at the nearby mall for exercise. Some days, Joe had to skip the walks because it made him too tired. When Joe drove out of town for night meetings, I noticed he came home exhausted.

He would say, "I'm going to take a shower and go straight to bed. I am so tired!"

When he started acting this tired, I encouraged him to let his doctor know how bad he was feeling.

Joe went for his heart checkup, and the doctor told him it was time for him to have the surgery. His blood pressure was too high, and he was at risk of having a heart attack.

"I would rather go ahead and have the surgery rather than wait around and have a heart attack," Joe bravely told the doctor.

Ready to face the surgery, Joe had the choice of an artificial valve or a pig's valve. Joe chose the artificial valve.

While doing the surgery at Shands Hospital in Gainesville, Dr. Martin found that Joe also needed a bypass. The bypass was performed as well as the artificial heart valve surgery.

After the operation, I saw Joe in the intensive care unit, and I just hurried back outside and cried. His face and body were so swollen that I wondered if he would live. My sons, Mark and Luke, questioned the doctor about the swelling, and he explained that this was normal for a patient to look badly swollen after this type of heart surgery. My sons and I were so relieved to hear the doctor's explanation for the swelling.

Without any complications, Joe healed nicely from the heart surgery. After a few weeks, he was working again. He was happy that the surgery was behind him. And he began to feel much better.

Every time we hear the song "Wind Beneath My Wings," it always had a lot of meaning for each of us.

The United Methodist Annual Conference was held in Lakeland with the bishop leading the sessions. There were hundreds of lay people as well as pastors present. Some of the business was interesting, some was boring. The music and entertainment were always good!

During a break at one of these yearly conferences, a lady walked up to the bishop and showed him a picture of her beautiful grandbaby. Joe looked at it with the bishop and said, "Bishop, now isn't that the ugliest baby you've ever seen?" The bishop looked shocked, and all he could say was "Joooooe!"

The bishop didn't know the lady was Joe's daughter-in-law's aunt. She knew Joe was joking. She had also been a member of one of his former churches. After she gave Joe a loving slap on the arm and told the bishop how they had known each other for years, a relieved grin came across the bishop's face. He said, "She is a beautiful baby."

Joe's mother was aging fast and showing signs of Alzheimer's disease. Her close friend Loraine told us about the problem, and we observed signs of her advancing condition when we visited her.

On a grocery shopping trip with Mother Grace, I watched her fly into a rage at the checkout lady for not checking her groceries fast enough. This was not the mild-mannered Grace who always had been patient and kind to everyone. She had never acted aggressive until now. She had been the perfect Southern lady.

At home, there were doors left unlocked, ovens left on after cooking, and other signs of strange forgetfulness.

It was time to take Mother Grace to the parsonage in Gainesville. She was no longer safe at home alone. Of course, she didn't like the idea of leaving her home, but she stubbornly agreed to go, and we had to promise that we would take her home often. Every day she asked, "When are we going home?" It didn't matter if we had just gotten back from Moultrie, the next day it was the same question. "When are we going home?"

Joe had another year of work before he could retire. On Sundays, he and I visited different churches in the district. One morning, as we were walking with Mother Grace from the parking lot of a large church, Mother Grace said, "Are we going to one of your nigger churches this morning?"

"Mother!" Joe was shocked. Hopefully, no one had heard her. From that morning on, Joe knew he couldn't take his mother to any of the black churches in the district. Before this strange disease, she had not used that type of language to describe people. Why now? One can never predict how their loved ones will change or what they might say as the disease progresses.

We decided it would be safe to take Mother Grace to arts and craft show. While we were there, we bought some ice cream cones and sat down on a bench to enjoy our ice cream. Mother Grace liked chocolate ice cream, so Joe got her a large cone.

Well, it was more than she wanted, so she just threw the half-eaten cone over her shoulder into the crowd of people walking by. Again, Joe was embarrassed in public, and all he could say was "MOTHER, you almost hit someone with your ice cream cone!" It didn't faze her; she just smiled. My reaction was to get tickled over the thought of someone almost getting hit in the face with a chocolate ice cream cone. Thank goodness no one was hit.

There were many small membership churches in the surrounding area of Gainesville. The conference did not have enough ordained, fully connected ministers to appoint to some of these churches. So the bishop gave Joe permission to appoint part-time lay ministers. Joe enjoyed doing this. Being familiar with each church, he knew the type of minister that each needed.

One appointment Joe made was a former priest. He had left the Catholic Church as a young man because it was not possible for him to marry the woman he loved and still serve in the priesthood. He and his wife worked as teachers and had raised four children in a Methodist church. The ex-priest made a wonderful pastor for a small membership church. It was a part-time weekend position, so he could continue his job as a teacher.

Another appointment Joe made was a deputy sheriff who had always wanted to be a pastor. He kept his deputy job and served a church too.

Then there was a retired dental surgeon who had gone to seminary as a young man. After seminary, he went to dental school, thinking he needed a better paying career to educate his large family. With the dental career behind him, he was ready to serve any church that needed him. Joe gave him a church, and he was great! Soon his small congregation grew much larger as people heard about his outstanding sermons.

Joe continued making appointments for those churches that couldn't afford a full-time minister. The churches were happy with their new pastors, and so was Joe. As the other district superintendents in the conference heard about Joe's successful appointments, they fondly called him Bishop Joe.

Joe and I made retirement plans as we took our walks around the neighborhood with our little dog, Rambo. The toy poodle had been with us since Stuart, and he loved taking walks with his masters. We talked about the house we bought in Moultrie down the street from Mother Grace's home. After retirement, we would try keeping Mother Grace happy in her home with hired help and us close by checking on her every day. Once we'd finished building our dream cottage at the farm, we planned to sell the house in Moultrie.

How our plans would work out, we didn't know. At this stage in life, plans could be made, but it's a waiting game to see how they'll work out. The important thing was having a good time making plans and being excited about each new decision. We must have bought dozens of magazines with different house plans and pictures.

Joe said, "It will be fun just mowing grass on the tractor at the farm. I'll restock the pond with fish. I'll enjoy grilling, and we can have picnics and fish fries for our friends and relatives. And I'll spend some time working at the local food bank. Checking on Mother every day will take a lot of time too."

I told him my plans, "I'll visit my relatives more often and enjoy my grandchildren. I'll invite friends and relatives for dinners. And I'll use my Stephen Ministry training to teach the program at our Moultrie church. I think it is special that we are going back to the church where we met and had our wedding. We might celebrate our fiftieth anniversary there in a few years."

While Joe and I were making our retirement plans, the ministers in the district formed a committee and planned a special retirement event for us. They asked me for the names and addresses of relatives and former church friends.

The date for the retirement event was set a couple of weeks before Joe's last annual conference in Lakeland. It was held at the Trinity United Methodist Church, which was Gainesville's largest Methodist church.

The committee kept lots of secrets from us about their plans. We had several surprises during the evening. They told us to wait at home for our ride to the church.

When Joe answered the doorbell, there stood a chauffeur in his black tux, and in the drive was a beautiful antique white Rolls-Royce!

"Your Highness, I'm here to take you and your lady to the church," the chauffeur said with a big grin.

"We're ready, but we didn't expect a ride like this," Joe said as he called to me that our ride had arrived. Our sons, Mark and Luke, had already taken Grandmother Grace to the church.

The car door was opened for me, and my hand was royally held as the chauffeur made sure I was comfortably helped into the back seat with Joe. The committee certainly had made plans for us to ride out in style. You would have thought we were going to a prom dance instead of a minister's retirement party.

We arrived at the church to find a minister and his wife waiting at the entrance with a king and queen capes for us. Over my little black formal dress, the red velvet cape was very striking. Joe looked like royalty in his new attire. With this dress surprise, we made our entrance down the long aisle.

From the back of the church, we saw a large banner across the stage that read "King and Queen of Moultrie." Then we saw the crowd, hundreds of people, our friends and relatives! As we made our way down the aisle, people stood and started clapping.

As we spied old friends along the end seats near the aisle, we stopped to shake their hands and give them hugs. The people continued clapping as we made our way to the special seats that were prepared for us on the stage.

After we were seated, the speeches began. A couple of local ministers in the district gave short welcome speeches.

Joe's former associate ministers, who now had churches of their own, told humorous stories about working with Joe. They each ended with a few compliments after roasting him good. There was lots of laughter. I was proud that my husband was remembered with such fondness.

Mark and Luke were given a chance to speak. They told how growing up in parsonages had shaped their lives. They complimented their mom and dad for giving them some special opportunities. My sister Evelyn also spoke, saying that we had shared our lives with my sisters in a special way. Joe had even influenced her daughter Pam's career choice. With our niece in seminary, we would have another Methodist minister in the family.

Our five grandchildren sang a special song in our honor. That was sweet.

God had blessed us with these talented children, and with grandparents' pride, we were bursting with joy!

After all the speeches, Joe and I responded with words of appreciation. Then everyone was invited to the reception party in the fellowship hall.

It was a special party with lots of good food and drinks for all. In a corner of the room was a large rotating screen showing the pictures of our wedding, our family, and different snaps of Joe at work, baptizing babies, performing weddings, and telling children's stories with George the Monkey.

People had come from each of our former churches. It had been almost forty years since we had come from Georgia to the Redland church in Homestead. Having people from there as well as Fruitland Park, Keystone, Lake Wales, Leesburg, Stuart, Ocala, and Gainesville was more than we expected. We stood in the receiving line a long time, shaking hands, hugging friends, and thanking them for coming. To have one's work and friendship remembered after so many years was very special.

With so many people to greet and thank, we had not been able to share time with our family. We not only had our children, we had other relatives from out of town. But the committee had thought of everything. They had arranged for us to have a late-night dinner party with our relatives at a restaurant.

Maybe this night was a new beginning instead of an ending. In retirement, there would be fewer people in our lives but more time for close friends and the people we loved the most, our family. We were going home again, back to Georgia. Life is always a progress, and we would continue telling ourselves, "Bloom where you are appointed!"

A WORD AFTER

JOE IS STILL the down-to-earth, friendly fellow he had always been. He loves to tease and joke with people all over town. Whoever gets to be in his company often will count him as a good friend. He now likes to dress casual all the time and seldom puts on a suit and tie. Almost every day he likes to leave town and go out to the farm and mow grass or do a little fishing. He loves the farm so much that his wife has a hard time getting him to go on a trip out of Georgia. He has reluctantly done a church service for nearby churches when a minister is sick or needs to go out of town. But he will not accept any full-time church work. He has changed from a workaholic to a laid-back retiree and does just what Joe wants to do. He did take a course in pine tree farming and now calls himself a tree farmer.

Joe's faith in God is a confident, deep faith that he feels when he is back to nature, fishing on the pond, cutting grass on the tractor, or taking walks to the river in the piney woods around the farm. People sense his faith when he shares a blessing at a picnic or dinner or anytime that he is called on for a blessing. His prayers are short and to the point.

How am I now? I think I am now a self-confident woman. I have an enjoyable and loving relationship with family and close friends. Looking back on life, I know that I've been able to make a difference in other people's lives. Some were big differences and some were casual differences such as a friendly greeting, a smile, or a warm handshake. I can feel good about some accomplishments in life, and I still have a strong spirit that will not let daily obstacles such as health issues keep me from reaching some of my present goals. I still enjoy giving a good party or attending one. I still like to shop for stylish clothes and dress neat. And I still have people say I look great, but I know the difference. For everyone, youth and beauty are fleeting, and I'm just trying to grow older gracefully.

WHAT DID I WANT OUT OF LIFE?

WHEN I WAS very young, I knew what I wanted out of life. I had my ambitions, my dreams, and my desires. I wanted a good education. I wanted fulfilling work. And most of all, I wanted a great family life. I wanted to share my life with others in a loving, Christian manner. The church and some faithful Christian people had raised me, and I knew I would always be loyal and faithful to my church. It does take a village to raise some children! In some of my childhood years, I lived near the marshes of Glenn with relatives and had the opportunity to dream and watch the marsh hens build their nest. From Sidney Lanier's famous poem, I remembered my favorite line that described my spiritual thoughts. I often thought, "As the Marsh-hen secretly builds on the watery sod, Behold I will build me a nest on the greatness of God."

WHAT DID I GET OUT OF LIFE?

IT SEEMS THAT people get what they expect from life or what they put into it. You sometimes do reap the seeds you sow. So far, I've had the experience of giving and receiving love with a faithful mate. I have experienced the love of children and the love of friendship. I have experienced the love of God! Like the Bible verse that says, "When I was a child, I thought as a child, but when I became an adult, I put away childish things" (1 Cor. 13:11). I am not as emotional with my religious thoughts and expressions as I was as a young person. I don't have all the answers, but I do know that my personal relationship with God has grown deeper and more mature over the years. I can count my blessings and know that God has touched my life with some special people and some very special experiences.

After all, I shared my life with my very own special minister.

Whether or not we bloomed well where we were appointed is a question only God can answer.

I for one feel as though it has been a wonderful life, and I thank him for it.

INDEX

J

James, William, 112-13
Jeanie (child heart patient), 86
Jones, Mary Alice, 29
Judy (adult Sunday school teacher), 21, 70

K

Kennedy, John F., 27, 31, 38
Keystone United Methodist Church, 38, 40
King, Martin Luther, Jr., 38, 113

L

Lam, Kim, 61, 82
Lam, Nguyen, 81-82
Lois (Gloria's sister), 15-16, 29-30, 33, 40,
    47-48

M

Man's Search for Meaning (Frankl), 114
Maureen (Gloria's friend), 94-95
McAuliffe, Christa, 87
McGill, Meg, 42-43
Morrison United Methodist Church, 78, 85

O

Oswald, Lee Harvey, 31

P

Pearson, Lee, 102

R

Rambo (toy poodle), 61, 98, 106, 118

S

Sam (pet Chihuahua), 76
Sara (Indian mother), 71-72
Smith, Grace, 34, 98, 100-101, 117-19
Smith, Hubert, 34, 100
Smith, Joe, 11-12, 24, 67, 78, 90, 97, 119
    appointment as Gainesville district
        superintendent, 108
    engagement and wedding, 12
    Fruitland Park appointment, 32
    heart valve problem and operation, 116
    Homestead, Florida, appointment, 24
    Keystone United Methodist Church
        appointment, 40
    Leesburg, Florida, appointment, 78
    ministry calling, 11
    ministry education, 11
    Ocala, Florida, appointment, 104
    retirement, 121
    retirement party, 119
    Stuart, Florida, appointment, 90
    TIA (transient ischemic attack), 101
    vacation in Anchorage, Alaska, 97
Smith, Luke, 28-29, 32-34, 36-37, 41-42, 48,
    65, 68-70, 74, 76, 84, 93, 100, 107,
    116, 119
Smith, Mark, 23-24, 26-29, 32-37, 41-42,
    44, 48, 52, 68, 70, 74, 76, 80, 82, 93,
    96, 100
Swainbom (retired dentist), 41, 46-47

T

Trinity United Methodist Church, 119
Turner, Ben, 19
Turner, Charles, 18-19

U

Upper Room, The, 75

W

LaVergne, TN USA
25 September 2009

158962LV00003B/29/P